Sabine Bösel • Roland Bösel
Lend me your ear and I'll give you my heart

Sabine Bösel ★ Roland Bösel

Lend me your ear and I'll give you my heart

The path to a happy love relationship

*This book is dedicated to all those couples
we were privileged to work with as therapists,
and from whom we were able to learn so much.*

Inhalt

🌱	A Matter of the Heart	9
1.	**Lend Me Your Ear and I'll Give You My Heart**	**11**
	A Voyage of Discovery in Each Other's Country	12
	Dialogue as a Bridge to Your Partner	16
	What It Was Really About	21
2.	**Where Love Falls**	**25**
	Soulmates	26
	What It Was Really About	33
3.	**You're so Different from Me**	**38**
	Fascinating, the Way You Are	39
	After the Sunshine Comes the Rain	40
	The Lost Self	41
	A Good Team—Recovering the Lost Self	45
	What It Was Really About	48
4.	**The Dynamic Duo**	**53**
	Minimizers and Maximizers	
	Two opposite temperaments	54
	The real issue	60
	The goal	61
	What It Was Really About	63
5.	**An Honest Look at Yourself before Presenting Your Partner with a Relationship Book**	**66**
	It's always me working on the relationship	67
	I had a difficult childhood	69
	My husband doesn't help with the housework	70
	Who is better – him or me?	71

	I'm not pretty enough	73
	Sexual assault	74
	He only ever wants one thing	75
	Men want to make us happy	76
	What It Was Really About	77
6.	**Discover Your Feelings for Your Own Sake; Your Wife Will Be Thankful**	**81**
	This endless emotionalism	82
	Like father, like son?	83
	I am doing it for my wife's sake	85
	I will only accept help when the water is up to my neck	86
	She spends hours talking about the same thing	87
	My childhood was perfect!	87
	My wife is so powerful	88
	Careful, this is a test	90
	What It Was Really About	91
7.	**A Thousand Reasons not to Talk to Each Other**	**94**
	The Space between You and Me	95
	Evasive Maneuvers	96
	Creating Awareness of Escape Hatches	100
	What It Was Really About	102
8.	**Finally, Someone Understands Me**	**105**
	The affair – A sign that something is missing in the relationship	106
	Clarifying instead of escaping	107
	Crises as the engine of development processes	113
	What It Was Really About	114
9.	**I Want to Become a Better Person for You**	**119**
	Embrace Conflict	120
	90:10 – The Twin Pack	120

	A Double Gift	121
	Unlearning and Learning—And Making Room for Something New	124
	What It Was Really About	127
10.	**Just Last Summer I Told My Wife that I Love Her**	**131**
	Love wants to be shaped and developed	132
	The Five Love Languages	135
	What It Was Really About	141
11.	**Sex, or The Simplest Thing in the World**	**144**
	The simplest thing in the world?	145
	Eroticism and sex	146
	What It Was Really About	158
12.	**Farewell Instead of Breaking Off**	**164**
	A Proper Farewell Provides a Basis for Something New	165
	Pain Is a Healing Form of Energy	166
	The Farewell Dialogue	167
	Letting Go of Each Other	171
	What It Was Really About	174
13.	**Had Children, Built a House, Planted a Tree—What Next?**	**177**
	Man strives as long as he lives	178
	How Do I Find My Couples Vision?	180
	Obstacles	183
	What It Was Really About	186
🌱	**Thank You**	**189**

A Matter of the Heart

Each couple has what it needs to be happy. This conviction is one of the most important foundations of our work as couples therapists. Nowadays, partners have too little contact with each other and don't invest enough time to get to know each other profoundly. Many of us think love is a matter of luck.

The most important decision of our lives was that we stuck it out despite the many hurdles we encountered. We've been a couple for the past forty years and have been working with couples for the past thirty. For about twenty years, we have been integrating the Imago Method into our work.

We feel very closely connected with Imago, as it comes in right at the point where our society lags in terms of appreciation and mindful communication in relationships. The methods and practices we offer we have tried on ourselves and still maintain; if you stick to them, it's a win-win for you, your relationship, and your children.

This book offers more than just scenes from our relationship. There are many beautiful and challenging love stories about the lives of others, meant to show how to overcome obstacles and let love unfold. We changed the names of the people concerned—and if you see yourself in their stories, it's pure coincidence and only proves that you are not alone in your problems.

Appreciation is another foundation of our work. We think it's wonderful that you are taking the time to read this book and that you want to do something for yourself and your relationship. We invite you to be appreciative of yourself and the important people in your life; this is especially true for your parents. Love relationships have a lot to do with our history, and specifically with our parents. However, this is not about blaming them for your present-day actions. We look into the past only to learn and grow.

Dear men and women, dear couples, regardless of your sexual orientation: our offer to provide you with the basis for a successful relationship and our many suggestions for how to achieve it—these come from the heart. We wish you many productive hours with this book, and the courage and persistence that will lead your love to a beautiful and happy future.

Sabine and Roland Bösel

1. Lend Me Your Ear And I'll Give You My Heart

A visit to the land of the other

A long, busy day draws to its end. Sabine has studied with the children all afternoon, gone to see the doctor with the little one and done the shopping for the birthday party the next weekend. When the children are finally in bed, she still has to tidy the kitchen, hoping that Roland will be home soon.

Around ten o'clock, Roland comes home, obviously exhausted, and throws his bag into a corner.

"I'm completely done in, today was simply too much. I'm going to watch some tv."

"Come on, really? You want to watch tv now? But I so wanted to tell you about my day!"

"I'm exhausted – do you really think this is the best time for me to sit down and talk?"

In the end, they do sit down together with a glass of wine, and Sabine begins to talk. Roland listens, yawning from time to time. Soon she drops a cue that prompts Roland to talk about himself. He gets into his stride and ends up telling her about his whole day. Sabine, who has not finished her story, is becoming more unfocused by the minute.

"I thought you wanted to watch tv, and now you're telling me everything about your day."

"I thought you wanted us to talk."

"True, but I hadn't even finished, and now you're telling me your whole story."

"Actually, I didn't feel like talking, but I still made an effort. And now I'd like to tell you something, and you aren't listening!"

Roland goes to the kitchen to get a glass of water. "In the kitchen there are crumbs all over the place. You know I don't like that."

"Now that's the last straw! First you don't want to talk, then you don't listen, and now you're accusing me of not doing the chores. Haven't you noticed how clean the apartment is? And you complain about a few crumbs!"

"And what about you? I come home completely done in, wanting to relax a little, and you absolutely have to talk. I'm talking all day anyway."

A Voyage of Discovery in Each Other's Country

According to a study, couples usually spend no more than two to four minutes a day discussing personal concerns. The rest of the time is spent exchanging various types of information regarding organizational matters, arguments, or power struggles. So, it's not surprising that there are so many divorces and separations, even though we've known for many years now about the positive effect of active listening, using "I" messages in conversation, and communicating with respect and appreciation. In professional careers, these insights acquired through communications research became standard practice long ago. But what about love relationships?

Carla and Frederic are a couple. Whenever she asked him to do something, and he answered, "Sure, in a minute," they argued. The reason? In Carla's country, "Sure, in a minute" means, "right away." But Frederic never fulfills her requests "right away." In his country, "Sure, in a minute" has a different meaning. At their therapy session, he said: "I thought you knew when I say that, it's my polite way of saying, 'Not now. I'll definitely do it, but only when it suits me.'" Two different worlds, two different customs.

It's the many little arguments like these that cloud everyday life. How often does our partner react strangely or overreact to what we consider an innocuous statement, so that we are left wondering? But very seldom do we investigate the background for such a reaction. So, these situations are repeated again and again without being solved. In some cases, the misunderstandings become so vast that a crisis is inevitable.

Love is not a state but an activity. You don't have to leave it to chance whether you're lucky in love or not. You can take it into your own hands by actively shaping your relationship. These steps include engaging with your partner and trying to understand his or her world. In this book, you'll find many suggestions. Here is one of the most important: Take a trip to your partner's country.

Relationship tourism

Just imagine you're taking a trip to a foreign country. How would you go about it? You'd try to make yourself familiar with the culture, language, and customs of that country. You don't want to act like a bull in a china shop or get in trouble with the law. In your country, if you carelessly drop a candy wrapper on the ground, chances are no one will react. If, however, you do the same thing in Singapore, you can be severely punished; different countries, different rules.

It's the same in your relationship. Your partner had different life experiences and learned different behavior patterns and views of life. Your partner had different parents and different caregivers than you did. That's how his or her character formed, distinctively and individually, just as your character is your own and no one else's.

If you don't want to act like a bull in a china shop in your partner's country, then why not take a voyage of discovery and learn about the culture, language, and customs? As we saw with Carla and Frederic, it's not a given that every word and behavior has the same meaning to all people. Why is that? Let's look at their background.

Carla came from a family that always made lots of plans, but no one ever took the first step to carry them out. Carla suffered through this, so, she subconsciously decided: When I grow up, if there is something that needs doing, I'll do it right away.

In Frederic's family, every plan was carried out to the last detail. Each family member had to help, and even as a child, he had little free time and hardly any breaks. He longed just to let himself go. He discovered that if he said to his mother, "Sure, right away," he could at least take a short breather. He has maintained that behavior to this day.

Pushing the curtain aside

The problem with conflicts and crises lies not in the issues themselves, but in the fact that they break the connection we have to one other. We wish that the other person would eventually turn into someone we'd like him or her to be, or that he or she would finally stop hurting us. But that doesn't lead us anywhere. Such demands only lead to broken communication.

Imagine two people sitting opposite each other, but there is a curtain drawn between them, blocking their view of each other.

They could move the curtain aside to re-establish contact, but they don't do it. This is what happens in breakups. They don't occur because one partner has a problem with the other one, but because they have lost contact with each other. That's the fundamental realization you need to move forward. Lend each other your ear, even if sometimes it isn't easy.

Martina and Gregor went to an Imago Couples Workshop, and a few days later to couples therapy. They had already set a divorce date, but wanted to understand why things had gone the way they did. They had three children and wanted to navigate the breakup successfully. They wanted to utilize the time before the divorce properly, or, as they said, spend the time having constructive conversations.

At the beginning of the session, both were quite tense, angry at each another, and desperate. We asked them to engage in a dialogue with each other. Martina expressed her great fear of divorce and of being treated unfairly. Gregor was irritated at first, but was eventually willing to listen. When Martina spoke about her childhood, how her father always demeaned her and she always felt like a fifth wheel, Gregor's eyes filled with tears because he now saw his wife in a different light. The connection was restored, and at that moment, there was no talk of divorce.

Half an hour later, we asked Martina to listen to Gregor. He told of his fear that Martina would throw him out if they kept arguing. That situation reminded him of his childhood, when he was sent to boarding school because his parents had major conflicts. There was no place for him in the family, and he still felt the same way.

"All I want is to feel safe with you and have my place. I don't even understand how the subject of divorce came up."

To travel through the other person's country and keep discovering new things requires a lot of attentiveness and openness to the fact that something surprising might arise at any time. Even if you have been married for twenty years or more, there's still a lot to learn about each other. We often think we know our partner well. On the other hand, we believe the other one knows what our needs are without having to say a word about them. Some people even think that not knowing your partner's wishes is evidence of a lack of love. But that's one of the biggest mistakes.

Dialogue as a Bridge to Your Partner

Talking to each other in everyday life can have many facets. Sometimes you listen more closely, other times less so, and you've probably caught yourself letting the other one talk while your mind is somewhere totally different. Our world is full of communication. We're constantly giving and receiving information. So, we think: "Oh, I just can't listen anymore, I've already heard enough!" Or: "How many times do I have to say the same thing over again?"

While our partner tells us something, we are already thinking: do I agree with that? How can I argue against it? How can I answer? What story from my own life does that remind me of? In effect, we are only listening with half an ear. We're not visiting the other person's country, but remaining in our own while we look for answers. So, we're missing a lot of valuable information that could bring us closer to our partner's country.

Especially when we're distressed or when it's a difficult topic, it's hard to listen attentively. As therapists, we then ask our couples to be fully aware when attending to one another. We offer them a couples dialogue. Similar to a visit to a foreign country, the dialogue ensures the necessary openness and appreciation to get closer to one another. The dialogue is designed so that only one person speaks at a time, and the other one pays attention, without assessing what was said or considering an answer.

Invitation to the dialogue

Actively shaping your relationship means that you keep extending invitations to each other: "Please lend me your ear for fifteen minutes, I want to tell you something." Or the other way around: "You look worn out. Do you want to tell me about your day?" Maybe you're thinking that's what you do regularly, anyway. But honestly, when your partner starts talking, do you really listen? Or do you let her talk for a while and then say something yourself, without really responding to your partner's story? Of course, that's also an option, but be aware of the fact that at the time, you weren't actually visiting your partner's country. You might have heard about her experiences, but not about what she felt and why she reacted this way, and not differently.

Having a dialogue

The most important thing in a couples dialogue is that talking, listening, understanding, and empathy are all separate from each other. As mentioned earlier, active listening, speaking in "I" messages, appreciation, and acknowledgment are the critical elements of communication. In couples dialogue, all of these elements are united.

The principle is as follows: the two partners sit opposite each other, as close as possible, and look into each other's eyes. It's agreed that one person speaks first, while the other listens. After a while, they can switch. The person speaking talks about an occasion, a problem, an irritation, a happy experience, or whatever topic arises. As a host in their country, they make sure that their counterpart understands everything well. The person listening is the attentive visitor. Their job is to listen and "mirror," that is, to repeat what was heard as precisely as possible.

The advantage of separating talking and listening is that one doesn't have to repeatedly change channels. The listening person only has to be in receiving mode. The speaker is solely in sending mode, which is a relief, as they each only have to concentrate on one thing at a time.

That doesn't mean that they have carte blanche. The person speaking is not allowed to verbally attack the listener. They must be aware of being the host, and must use a language that the guest can understand and accept. The listener, on the other hand, should keep all their wisdom, interpretations, ideas, and adversities to themselves. They should be aware of being a guest in another country, where they can get to know other cultures and customs, maybe even learn something about themselves and break down their prejudices.

Having conscious couples dialogues takes a little practice. And when the issues are difficult ones, for example, when you are fighting or are in the midst of a serious crisis, you will probably need the assistance of experienced therapists to succeed in dialogue. We've provided some exercises for you at the end of this chapter, with which you can try out the dialogue.

The power of dialogue

An essential part of Imago Couples Dialogue is active listening by repeating as precisely as possible what the other person has said. If you say to your wife: "I'm so frustrated that you have to go away for three days," and your wife says: "I heard you say that you're frustrated that I have to go away for three days," she mirrored you perfectly.

You might think it's a pretty strange way of speaking. Probably everyone feels the same way, the first time they are confronted with the principle of active listening. And it certainly would be strange if you asked your husband: "Darling, where did you park our car?" and your husband mirrored you by saying: "I heard you asking where I parked our car. Did I get you?" Such a situation requires nothing but a straightforward answer.

But if you want to address an important topic, then mirroring is an excellent tool for improving understanding and closeness. Brain research offers a good explanation of why this works. Researchers have discovered that someone being mirrored finds it easier to relax. It provides security and creates trust so that one is willing to dive deeper into the topic.

When Verena and Peter came to our office, Peter had severe burnout syndrome. He was head of a large company and thought it would be good idea to do couples therapy, as an entire workshop would take up too much time that he didn't have. At the session, we asked Verena to mirror him. Peter protested. "That takes too much precious time; besides, I'm the one paying the bill here, and what good is it if someone just repeats what I say?"

Finally, he agreed, and Verena mirrored what she heard while looking into his eyes. "Did I get all of that?" she asked at the end. "You heard most of it," Peter said. "I also said that I have the feeling my time is just running through my fingers, and with all the work, there's nothing for me. All I do is function." Verena mirrored his words, and suddenly, Peter's eyes widened. "I don't know why, but suddenly I feel incredibly sad, and I'm afraid to really feel it," Verena mirrored. "You got me," Peter said, "and now that I've said that, I also feel ashamed." He was silent for a while, and then tears suddenly ran down his cheeks. "I have no idea why I'm crying," he said, "but it feels good. I haven't cried for thirty years."

Weeks later, Peter told us that only through Verena's attentive listening did he feel the security he needed. It was the only way he could unpack his deepest feelings. Peter was so impressed by the powerful effect of mirroring that he even introduced this technique to his company.

The goal is mutual benefit

If two people disagree, we usually consider compromise as the best possible solution. However, a compromise requires both to give something up. So, we think it's more important to find a mutual benefit that doesn't take something away from anyone, but rather, brings something new to both.

Imagine two thick ropes knotted together. If we cut the knot, all that's left at both ends is disconnected pieces. They're lost. It's the same with compromise. When a couple in a crisis comes to us with the idea that a quick breakup is the best solution, it's like the cut knot. Each one has lost something, and each is left holding a useless piece of rope. But if the couple connects and a dialogue begins, then it is as if this knot is carefully untied, and both ropes remain intact. Then, both of them can decide how their lives should continue.

What It Was Really About

The scene at the beginning of this chapter clearly describes what happens when two partners come from different countries. In Sabine's country, multi-tasking is the issue: work, children, household. In Roland's country, the issue is a busy therapy practice, with time for his children only during lunch break.

"When we got together in the evening, each of us was still trapped in their own country. Only because we, as therapists, know how important it is to listen to one another, did we both make an effort. But we were tired and unable to concentrate. We were unable to visit each other's country."

Then the first fighting words fell: "You're not listening!" And the nagging because of a few crumbs was the last straw—basically, a typical situation both Roland and Sabine were well familiar with, because listening was not really a priority. In Sabine's family, important matters were usually swept under the carpet, or only discussed when those involved were absent. In Roland's family, the main topic of discussion was the family business. There was little room for personal matters.

"We should have made an agreement about who listens to whom, and when," Roland said. "And I could have said: 'Sabine, my dear, I'm tired, but I can see it's important for you to tell me something. I suggest we take half an hour in which you can tell me everything, and I'll pay close attention. And tomorrow evening, we'll do it the other way around: I can talk, and you listen.' That would have helped us to pay attention. We could have understood each other better, and both would have benefitted. But as it was, we ended our busy day with an argument, which cost us even more energy."

What You Can Do

🌱 Try a mini-dialogue. Invite your partner to take part in an experiment. Take two chairs and sit facing each other, without a table or anything else between you. Relax your body, that is, don't fold your arms, and maintain eye contact.

Use a timer—each of you is allowed to talk for five minutes, while the other one listens. Decide who speaks first and start with a simple subject. For example, I saw an older man in the subway who made me feel sad. Or: I had a funny dream last night. Or: I saw a film yesterday that touched me deeply. All of these are subjects that aren't very ambitious to begin with, to ensure that your first dialogue is successful.

Agree on each saying a sentence the other one mirrors, beginning with: "I heard you saying….", and ending with, "Did I get that?" When the sender feels he was correctly understood, he answers: "Yes, you got me." If something important is missing, you say: "You got most of that, but what's also important that you get, is…" And whatever is missing is mirrored again. After five minutes, you switch, regardless of the outcome.

After the two five-minute sessions, you both say: "The most important thing I got out of this conversation with you is…." It should be something constructive, nothing negative. Again, both parties should mirror this.

In the end, each of the parties should express appreciation for the other one, for example: "It felt so good that you listened to me with open, loving eyes." Or: "I'm so glad

that you told me about your experience in the subway, that you were so moved by it, and you let me see your tears."
Take at least an hour to mull over these mini-dialogues before you continue talking about them.

🌱 A crisis is often the result of important topics that have been avoided for too long between two people who are close to each other. Look for an Imago Therapist you feel confident with and, above all, be patient. Things took a long time to get shoved under the rug, so it will take some time to uncover them and resolve them properly.

🌱 Discover yourself. Take two chairs again and prepare everything as described for the "mini-dialogue." Set the timer for thirty minutes and invite your partner to visit you. Choose an issue that has been on your mind lately, even if it has nothing to do with your partner.
Instead of describing the problem in detail, use the thirty minutes to figure out how this topic is connected with your history, childhood, or youth. Even if nothing comes up right away, allow yourself those thirty minutes. For the visiting partner, it's important to be open. Even if you hear something you do not understand at all, mirror it lovingly and without further comment.
End the dialogue as described above.

🌱 We often receive recognition or appreciation from our partner without realizing it. Therefore, we suggest the following exercise:
Agree that for seven consecutive days, each of you will

show appreciation or regard for the other, like commenting on something they did or a way that they behaved. Don't say it in passing, but so that what you say is really heard. Ask your partner to mirror the appreciation.

Voice your appreciation, regardless of the daily situation, even if you're not on the best terms at the moment. And in case your partner forgets, give them the chance to make up for it by doubling up the next day.

2. Where Love Falls

My partner is right, no matter what

It's dusky in the living room. Sabine turns on the desk lamp and packs documents into a large shoulder bag. As she gets ready to go, Roland comes in.
"When are you coming back?" he asks.
Sabine rolls her eyes. "Don't know," she answers and shoulders the bag.
"Are you starting with that again? You always answer 'I don't know.' But I want to know when you're coming home!"
"We have to work and..."
"Not that again," Roland interrupts. "Last time, all you did was gab for hours. You call that work?"
"Right. We gabbed, but before that, we worked. I won't let you spoil my therapy training! I'm leaving!"
"You'll stay, and we'll talk!"
Sabine puts her bag back on the desk and shakes her head. "You're like my mother. I won't be locked up! I worked hard all day."
"Worked? What do you mean by 'worked'? I know the meaning of work. I've been on my feet since four this morning, and now it's seven in the evening, and I'm dead tired. First I was in the meat factory, then shopping at St. Marx, and in the afternoon in the store at the cash register. And what are you doing? You sit at your desk. And now you want to go out and have fun?"
Roland is bewildered and furious. He wants Sabine to stay home tonight. But she remains silent and rummages in her bag with-

out searching for anything in particular. She's angry, and all she wants is to get away as fast as possible.

"I'm leaving!" she says, and slams the door behind her.

Roland is left behind, agitated, and immediately dives into his work. That helps to distract him from nagging thoughts: Is Sabine really meeting with colleagues? Just recently a man walked her home, quite a likable one at that!

After work, while Sabine tells her girlfriends about the fight with Roland, he's in bed, unable to fall asleep. Like poison, the fear that Sabine no longer loves him eats away at his thoughts.

Sabine comes home very late. Tired and weary, she climbs into bed. "Where have you been for so long?" he explodes.

Sabine remains silent. But Roland sticks to his guns, and so they argue and argue until finally, in the early morning hours, they embrace and fall asleep.

Soulmates

Each relationship that lasts longer than six months suggests a kinship of souls. Whom we choose as a partner is no coincidence: There's something familiar about them, even if we're only aware of it subconsciously. Especially in the first phases of falling in love, we use phrases like: "It's as if we've known each other forever." Or: "You seem so familiar to me."

This person reveals the good things we've experienced in our life so far, and especially in the first months of getting to know and love each other, we're ecstatic about the special bond in which we experience so many beautiful, exciting and at the same time secure moments.

But they also reveal the painful ones. Together we might experience unimagined happiness, but it can also leave us deeply hurt. We experience this when falling in love moves on to the next phase in the relationship, when the butterflies in the stomach fade, and everyday life takes over. That's when difficult situations might arise, conflicts break out, or power struggles set in. It's exhausting, and when it gets too much for us, we reach for the first best solution: We solve the problem by separating. Then we hear: "He hurt me so much, I don't want to go on living with such a person." Or: "She became like a stranger." Or: "We just drifted apart."

At first, a breakup is a relief, because the arguments stop and you can finally breathe easy again. Months later, however, we find out that the difficulties were only a fraction of the partnership, and we separated from a person who was so familiar to us. Perhaps we're in a new relationship and are frustrated to find out that the same problems arise again. All we did was exchange the person, but we kept the problems.

Mirror, mirror on the wall

The bond between you and the person you chose as a partner is no accident. It's deeper than you realize at first glance. Your subconscious makes sure that you fall in love with someone you're not only optically attracted to, but who's also compatible with your inner life. Your psyche is the result of all your positive and negative life experiences. The person you fall in love with might have experienced different things than you, but they lead to the same life topics. Your subconscious chooses according to these criteria, so there is a good chance that you will face the same problems when you switch partners.

Here's an example:

Lena came to us for therapy because she and her husband Kurt had drifted apart after two years of marriage and the birth of a daughter. When Kurt slapped her in the face after another recurring quarrel, she drew the line. During a therapy session she said the following: "When I was a child, my mother beat me, and I certainly don't want to live with a man who also beats me." Lena and Kurt separated.

Half a year later – Lena was still in therapy – she fell in love with Fabian. "He's so different," she gushed. "He's as soft and kind-hearted as a lamb." Eight months later, the first love rush was over, first conflicts arose, and during a quarrel, Fabian hit Lena. What does that tell us? One of Lena's central topics is violence. Her mother beat her, humiliated her, and even locked her in the basement. As an adult, for the second time, she had chosen a man for whom violence was also an issue. Both Kurt and Fabian had experienced beatings in their childhoods.

Lena left Fabian. "I've had enough of men," she said, and stayed single for the next two years. Then Jakob arrived. Here, too, there were conflicts in the relationship, but they could be solved, and there was no violence. Lena became pregnant, and they had a daughter: Lena's second, Jakob's first child. When the little daughter was six months old, new conflicts arose. Lena accused Jake of preferring their child to Lena's first daughter. As a result, Jakob refused to talk to her for a few days, which made Lena so furious, that she yelled at him, and in her despair she hit him.

She came to the therapy session terribly ashamed of herself. "That's how my mother must have felt," she said. "I have to resolve this issue with my mother, or I'll always carry it around with me!" Lena's mother refused to come to therapy, so Lena and Jakob decided on couples therapy. Both of them were able to resolve the issue of violence, since such assaults were nothing new to Jakob, as it turned out. To this day, ten years later, they stay in touch with us by writing how happy they are to have worked out and resolved this difficult life issue. They argue sometimes, but have found a way to handle the situations constructively.

We can't escape from our problematic life issues. Even if, in the moment of conflict, breaking up seems like a relief and the most obvious solution, we recommend entering into a dialogue first, and making further decisions only afterward.

Prince Charming and the Dream Girl

The kinship of souls is reflected by the fact that although we have had different childhood experiences, we have retained similar positive and negative emotions. "Then why don't we pick someone who represents only the positive parts of childhood?" This is a question we're asked again and again. Well, in a way we do just that. But in the getting-to-know-each-other phase, when we are falling in love, we primarily see the positive things. During this phase, we believe in the Prince Charming or the Dream Girl. We only show our best selves—the "chocolate-coated" side. Negative behavior is blocked out, or at least not perceived as such.

"Sure, I noticed that she was prickly," one of our clients said once, "but there were so many good sides to her that it didn't bother me at all. Now that characteristic really bothers me, and I ask myself why I got involved with this woman. Looking back, I can say that the positive energy was so strong that I fell in love, with the hope that she might lose her prickliness."

Our Imago Trainer, Hedy Schleifer, once told us: "We humans would long be extinct if it weren't for this infatuation, when we see things through rose-colored glasses." If we noticed only the aggravating, problematic sides, it would be hard to fall in love.

There are two sides to every story. We have no problem with the positive things we have in common. It's the negative life issues that bother us, that rob our energy and make life difficult. We often suppress the negative experiences of our childhood or forget them, and it's uncomfortable when our partner holds up a mirror with their behavior.

The zebra effect

To humans, all zebras look the same: like a horse with stripes. However, a baby zebra knows the exact difference between the stripes of its mother and those of other zebras. Why? Because, to ensure its survival, it's essential for the baby zebra to find its mother immediately. She's the only one providing protection. Only she will feed it, and only she will risk her life to protect her offspring when a lion attacks. So, the baby zebra has a barcode saved, for which it scans all the other zebras to find its mother.

It's quite similar with us humans when we grow up. Depending on how we are nurtured, raised, and socialized, a sort of barcode is imprinted on our brains. It consists of many experiences: the way we were loved by our caregivers, or hurt, or neglected by them. Each line of that code is related to an experience. Later on, we subconsciously feel drawn to people with a similar bar code. If there is enough agreement, it will turn into love. If there is too little, the relationship will not outlast the first six months of infatuation.

Human nature demands that we grow and evolve, make discoveries and, if required, change our behavior. This is only possible thanks to the principle of the matching barcodes; it's the negative atmospheres, experiences, and traumas that want to be resolved and healed. They are stored within us, and only by encountering others can we become aware of them, and it is only what we are aware of that can be changed.

Pushing the right buttons

"You cannot heal what you do not feel," they say, and that's why our partner is the ideal person to help us learn and evolve. Of all the people around us, they are best able to find our sore points, so that all the old traumas and negative experiences rise to the surface and become perceptible.

We should actually be grateful to our partner for finding the right buttons. They push, and we jump—and at the same time, we start pushing their buttons. Anyone who divorces at that point is throwing away many opportunities. If, however, the partners sit down together and investigate their backgrounds, they help each other to heal.

Maria and Toni came to us for couples therapy. Maria was frustrated because Toni often created a bad mood. "All day long I'm looking forward to the evening together. Then he comes home, is in a bad mood, and it's all about his fears and aches and pains. That's not very erotic, is it?" A subsequent Imago Dialogue made it possible for Toni to understand how Maria felt. Maria told him how painful it had been for her that her mother was always so negative. For her as a child, being at home was always connected with a gloomy atmosphere.

So, when Toni comes home from work in a bad mood, he

pushes "the right button" for Maria. Without her childhood experience, she could have been much more relaxed about Toni's behavior. Maria could have laughed it off and gone back to normal. Instead, she reacted and the conflicts took their course.

Accepting the power of the kinship of souls

The power of the kinship of souls helps you to examine, decipher, and resolve your barcodes, step-by-step together. Of course, that's no guarantee, but in the long run, it can be an efficient way for you to cope with your recurring problems. Once, after couples therapy, a man said to his wife: "Now that I'm free to leave you, because I have become so aware and clear about everything, I'm also free to stay with you. Now I can experience new things with you and don't have to keep repeating my old paradigms."

Stick to it even if your conflicts are great ones. Do it for yourself, your children, and your partner. So many sons and daughters would have wished for their parents to have reflected consciously on their relationship! One of our clients once said: "Today I'm glad that my parents split up. I don't think it would have been possible to stay together. But if they had been willing to look at their issues together and process them, to reflect on what led to the split and to forgive each other, then I know my life would have been different and happier."

What It Was Really About

In the scene at the beginning of the chapter, Sabine and Roland are going through a power struggle: Sabine's goal is freedom. She doesn't want to be confined by Roland. She needs to feel that she can evolve. As he won't accept that, she leaves him behind with his resentment and unhappiness.

Roland is also battling each time Sabine leaves. His goal is to have Sabine nearby because only in the vicinity of his loved ones can he recharge his batteries. He criticizes her, accuses her of infidelity, and refuses to accept her work for what it is.

Dear readers, you're probably thinking: How can that ever work out when these two have such completely opposite goals? One of them needs freedom, the other one closeness? Well, Sabine and Roland's relationship was on a rollercoaster for a while. But in the end, they took a close look at the reasons for their behavior and realized they genuinely are soulmates.

"I was an overprotected child," Sabine explains, "probably because something really terrible happened before I was born. My sister, Ursula, fell from the window of our apartment and died." A year later, when Sabine was born, everyone was thrilled. Her father once told her: "And then you arrived, and things were fine again." But how can the birth of one child make up for the death of another one? In a way, Sabine was functionalized. She was looked upon as a replacement for her sister, and it was her job to cheer up her mother instead of just being herself.

"My mother went everywhere with me, and was always exceedingly careful; she watched every step I took with eagle eyes," recounted Sabine. It goes without saying that this was the reason she reacted so sensitively when Roland tried to infringe on her freedom. "As a child, I constantly felt this atmosphere of sadness, pain, and guilt. I learned that closeness was something stressful and depressing; I urgently need freedom."

As a child, Roland's needs and fears were not noticed either. His parents, besides having four children, had to operate a large butcher's business. They were so preoccupied with their work that there was very little time for cozy family get-togethers.

"I felt very alone," Roland said. "I was extremely happy when my mother was around, and it was harrowing for me every day when she left me alone again to go to work. It always felt like an eternity before she returned home."

Now you can imagine why Roland reacted so sensitively when Sabine repeatedly went out to work with her colleagues in the evening. "I learned that my needs are only met when someone is with me. I didn't have confidence that Sabine would come back, so I reacted with alarm when she left."

Both Sabine and Roland had loving parents. However, they did not get enough nurturing attention. Their fears and desires were never noticed enough. That's the deep kinship of souls connecting them. Only the strategies they both developed were different. By realizing their kinship, they learned to understand each other and meet each other in the middle.

What You Can Do

Individual exercises

🌱 Pay attention to yourself for two or three days, to observe which issues concern you especially; maybe even upset you. Where do you place your attention? For example, when out on a walk you might notice a crying child more readily than the trees blooming by the side of the road. Jot down your observations and glance at your notes again a couple of days later. Group similar issues together. Could these issues date from your childhood or youth? What issues did you encounter in the first years of your life? Find someone you know who you can talk to. Take care that this is a person who treats you lovingly and above all, listens to you instead of giving you advice. Ask the person to listen to you and possibly mirror you (see Chapter 1).

🌱 List the times of crisis in your life. Name them and organize them approximately by date. Start with the present and go back to your birth. You can use what you remember or what you were told.
Then think about how the crisis changed your life or how you evolved. What has stayed the same and is still repeating itself?

🌱 Look at your previous relationships. Which issues that you might know from your childhood or youth are repeating themselves in your current relationship? This is not so much about real situations that repeat themselves, but rather about the issue embedded in them. For example,

I often argue with my partner about money. In my family of origin, there was an abundance of money. For him, money was also an issue, but because there wasn't enough of it.

🌱 Do I know my so-called trigger words? Trigger words are terms to which we respond inappropriately, by being defensive of an attack. Examples can include:
"Do you love me?"
"When will we finally get married?"
"We should visit my parents again."
"It's time to tighten your belt."
"I want to know what you think."
"Work first, then play."
"You're not listening to me."
"You're like…"
"You don't want to sleep with me."
"It's always about sex."
Make your own list and then explore: What injuries and unpleasant experiences are causing you to react so strongly today?

Exercises together

🌱 Ask your partner to talk with you about all the deliberations, thoughts, and experiences you had. Always choose only one issue per talk.

🌱 Take half an hour and tell your partner about the wonderful experiences you had in your childhood. Which caregivers were especially nurturing and supportive, and who were your role models? If you have a photo album, show your partner photos from your childhood and youth.

🌱 Visit places together that were important in your childhood or youth. This may include playgrounds or schools, vacation sites, or homes you lived in. Tell your partner what it was like for you to have been there. What was good, what was perhaps difficult? This is a way of showing your partner the outer world you lived in, giving them the opportunity to understand and experience your inner life.

3. You're so Different from Me

Opposites attract

Roland and Sabine have been a couple for only a few months and are planning their first vacation together.
"I want to go somewhere just to relax. Enjoy the sun, beach, ocean, sit in a café and drink a cappuccino…"
"Really? I'd love to go to Rome. It's so full of culture, so much history to explore. I bet you'd like it, too."
They talk about it for a while, and finally, Sabine succeeds in catching Roland's interest. They go to Rome. Equipped with travel guides, they visit the Sistine Chapel, St. Peter's Cathedral, the Trevi Fountain, the Spanish Steps, and many other beautiful sights there.
"I'm overwhelmed," is Roland's comment on the third day. "I never would have thought how great it could be to discover a city on a vacation. Even though I'm dead tired, I'm happy. Thank you for talking me into coming here."
Sabine is in her element. On the fourth day of the vacation, she suggests visiting the Santa Maria Maggiore Church.
"Come on, Sabine, you're not serious. It's 40 degrees centigrade in the shade, and you want to climb up that hill? Ten horses couldn't drag me up there!"
"If I tell my mother that I didn't see that church, she'll flip."
"Still. Can't we just rest today?"
Sabine agrees, and they stroll along the shopping streets, go with the flow, sip coffee on Piazza Navona, and hang out.
"What a great day that was," Sabine comments during dinner in

a cozy tavern in the evening. "So relaxing. It was never like that at home!"

Fascinating, the Way You Are

Veronica and her friend were on a hiking trip in the Tyrolean Mountains, when they met Werner in a cabin. They discovered that they had planned the same route for the following day, and the three of them started their journey. Werner walked silently ahead of them, while the two women chatted now and then. Halfway there, they had to cross a steep snowfield. At first, Veronica hesitated. She was afraid of slipping and wanted to turn back, but finally, let herself be talked into continuing.

Werner went first so that Veronica could easily step into his footprints, but in the middle of the field, she became frightened. "I'm not taking another step, or I'll slip!" Werner turned and went back toward her. "Don't look down!" he shouted to her. "Just keep your eyes on me." When he reached her, he took her hand and led her, step-by-step, safely to the other side of the snowfield.

Later in the cabin, the trio was happy about the outcome of the difficult situation. Especially Veronica and Werner got along great. Veronica glowed with happiness and charm, and after a couple of glasses of schnapps, she even began to sing. Werner was reserved, but he enjoyed her company and was happy listening. He seemed proud to have saved this bundle of spirit in the snowfield. Veronica, too, was enthralled by her hero.

This is how falling in love can happen. In a challenging situation, two people get to know each other's qualities. One is fascinated by the calmness of the other one, which she herself would never have been able to muster. The other is thrilled by the playful disposition that he wouldn't have permitted himself.

After the Sunshine Comes the Rain

A participant at one of our Imago Couples Workshops responded to the question of what comes after falling in love with "disenchantment." They continued, "At first, everything is just perfect, and then it turns out that there's a catch to it." We call that phase after falling in love, the power-struggle phase. After floating on cloud nine for a while, differentiation begins— getting to know each other more deeply. Characteristics and behavior patterns we initially idealized are now perceived in their various facets, and often, this is when the power struggle begins, in which both of you want to stake out territory. The first throes of love blinded us in a way that now, utterly sober, we're sure that, most likely, we have chosen the wrong partner.

That's what happened to Werner and Veronica. Three years after their wedding, they asked for a couples therapy appointment.

"I can't take it anymore," Veronica said. "Usually, I'm the first one home. Then, when Werner comes home, he'll say maybe ten words to me all evening. He'd rather watch TV." Veronica talked and talked. And what did Werner answer? "What more is there to say? Veronica already said everything. This woman talks constantly!"

The Lost Self

Everyone is born with a unique life energy. In Imago Therapy, we call it core energy. We're all equipped with positive characteristics: Liveliness, curiosity, intelligence, creativity, empathy, gentleness, temperament, love for experimentation, serenity, trust, ambition, thoughtfulness, and so on. We want to experience the world as a whole and develop with all of our abilities. And because we're equipped with all the fundamental characteristics, we have the potential to do so.

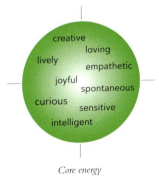

Core energy

A baby, for example, has the potential to learn to walk. It crawls, and one day it will be able to coordinate all of the approximately sixty muscles that will enable it to stand up and take the first steps. This experience is stored in the brain as a model to be reproduced later on. Of course, this baby needs not only these physical abilities to learn to walk, but also a social environment that provides appropriate stimuli.

This holds true for everything we learn as children. We are all endowed with psychological attributes, but some things get lost during upbringing, because we are supported and encouraged in some things, and restrained or even prevented in others. For example, we all have the potential to think and act. As a result of its upbringing one child will learn to think before acting, whereas another learns to respond spontaneously without taking much time to think.

The four fields of core energy

Our core energy evolves into four fields: thinking, feeling, acting, and applying the five senses. Depending on our upbringing certain areas are encouraged, and others impeded so that they are scarcely developed, or even stunted. The sum of the energy remains the same, but the focal points develop differently.

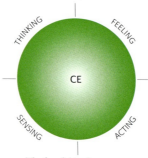

The four fields of core energy

This education—or upbringing—is partly due to role modeling and partly due to messaging. "Think before you speak," is an example of a message that aims to stimulate the act of thinking, as is: "That's great! What lovely stories you make up!" When parents or relatives give books as presents or answer questions readily, they help a child train the thinking muscle.

Feelings are trained in messages like, "It's okay to be scared," or, "I'm glad you show your feelings," or, "It feels good to cry," or, "I can understand that you're angry." Children, who are motivated to act, hear messages like this: "That's great!" or, "I like the way you dance in front of the mirror!" They will be encouraged to try out new things and are supported in doing so.

Children who could fully develop their feelings were allowed to "eat what you like," "Take as much as you want!" To be told, "You smell good!" or "I don't like this music, but if you like it, I'm happy for you to," are further examples for messages that nurture emotions.

At the same time, there are parent messages that hinder development in certain areas. "Leave thinking to the horses, they have a bigger head!" could, for example, encourage a child to not lend much thought to issues coming its way. A message along the lines of "High spirits are seldom a good thing" might teach a child to keep its feelings in check and practice emotional restraint.

"Don't climb up there, or you'll fall!" is certainly no encouragement to train physical dexterity and reflexes, nor is, "Can't you sit still?" And messages like: "Eat your soup, it's not too spicy," or, "Don't stare at people," limit children in testing their five senses and trusting in them. Limitations—as well as encouragement—can occur even without verbal messages, when parents have more or less pronounced characteristics in their own lives and children copy their behavior.

In case you, dear reader, are inclined to bemoan your fate because your parents inflicted so many prohibitions or constraints, please remember: parents are just people. It would be unjust to ask parents to promote their children equally in all areas. You parents were children once, too, whose parents in turn also limited or supported them in certain areas. In this way, behavior patterns are passed down through the generations. Sometimes during a generation change, a model can be reversed entirely. This might happen if, for instance, parents are extreme in acting out their intellectuality, and as a child, one wants more than ever to do the opposite, by acting before thinking. In any case, strengthening or limiting a core energy is part of a family pattern.

Each of us goes through life and encounters other people with all these encouraged and restricted areas. We feel a unique attraction to some people because they are soulmates or because they reinvigorate areas that are stunted in us. Not only similarities attract, but opposites as well.

Pot and lid

With Veronica and Werner, the contrasts are quite apparent. Veronica is lively and bubbly and openhearted. Werner is calm, remains collected under challenging situations, and keeps a cool head. In the beginning, Veronica is thrilled about her lifesaver, and Werner is fascinated by the woman who fills his life with liveliness and freshness. Three years later, they criticize precisely the things that attracted them initially. Veronica complains that Werner stopped talking to her. She'd like to know how his day at the office went, but he doesn't want to talk about it, because he wants to take a break from the problems of his professional life. He prefers to withdraw to avoid his wife's torrent of words.

"There's nothing fun about our relationship anymore. We used to take wonderful hikes, now nothing at all happens anymore," she comments.

Werner, on the other hand, complains about Veronica talking so much and getting so emotional. "If I tell her about my job, she wants to go on talking about it for hours, possibly even giving me tips. I don't give her tips about what she can improve in her job, and if so, then I offer a solution rather than forever picking the problem apart. I'd rather withdraw and read or watch TV. I can't stand all those emotions," he said.

Werner and Veronica have evidently reached the power-struggle phase. In their infatuation phase, they were enthusiastic about those characteristics in each other that had been stunted in themselves. But the longer they were together, and their infatuation gave way to everyday life, the more often they reacted irritably or with hostility.

During a power struggle, we become aware of what we lost. The typical reaction: We want to get our partner to the point where they forego the part that is stunted in us. As we weren't allowed to live that potential, we want to confine them as well. We do this in such a way that, for example, we transmit the same limiting messages to our partner that we received from our parents—maybe not with the same words, but surely with the same intention.

A Good Team—Recovering the Lost Self

Nature means us well. It makes sure that we choose a partner who mirrors our lost self and provides us with the opportunity of finding it again—as long as we are prepared to accept that partner as coach and model. However, it becomes tragic when, instead, we criticize and devalue them for those characteristics and behaviors. Unfortunately, that's precisely the phase where breakups take place.

Fortunately, Veronica and Werner decided not to give up so quickly, but to look at the matter more closely. Veronica's core energy was primarily molded by her mother, who demonstrated that it's good to show emotions. The mother was a lively, emotional woman. Veronica experienced a mother who was quite happy, but also overly anxious, especially concerning her daughter. She found it difficult, sometimes, to pause, stop and think, keep a cool head and realistically assess any actual risk.

Werner's emotional world was restricted when he was a child. His older sister liked to call him "scaredy-cat," and his nanny taught him that boys aren't allowed to be afraid. "Just look at your sister, she's not even scared like you, a boy!" Werner learned to suppress his feelings.

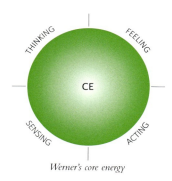

Werner's core energy

After three years of marriage, Veronica and Werner have a problem with their differently developed core energies—but they are still a good team. In those areas where one was suppressed, the other had strength, and vice versa. All in all, they're a well-rounded package with all of their energies developed. If they manage to appreciate each other's assets instead of devaluing them, and if they can use their abilities constructively for themselves and for their relationship, they will make a wonderful team. Then they will have fulfilled all the prerequisites needed for being successful as parents, in their professions, in their characters, and as a couple.

Acceptance and appreciation have a positive side effect. If Veronica stays true to her developed energies, Werner may be able to dig up his buried qualities and re-learn them, and vice versa. This, of course, only works if we realize that we chose our partner precisely because he or she is talented in those areas, which are stunted in us. Look at your partner as a coach who can help you to recover your lost self.

Learning in small steps

This learning process might, of course, take some time, because if you haven't used a particular ability for a long while, that "muscle" has to be built up slowly. A couch potato won't turn into a marathon runner overnight. Someone restricted in their thought processes won't have an easy time writing a book. Someone who was limited in her actions won't be able to harness all of her physical skills right away, and someone whose sensations were dampened won't immediately be enthusiastic about trying out every international dish. Finally, someone whose emotional muscle was stunted won't be able to allow himself to feel and show fear easily. All of those things must slowly be re-learned, and it takes a lot of willpower, patience, and perseverance, as well as the ability to accept setbacks. And their partners will also need patience and love to support that learning process and to praise even the small steps.

Veronica and Werner jointly decided to participate in an Imago Couples Workshop. During one of the breaks, they told us: "We are so shocked to find out about the correlations we discovered here. Now we understand why we had to downgrade each other's assets. We are almost ashamed of the way we treated each other, because those assets, those energies are exactly what we love about each other." Instead of separating or putting up with things, they became aware which mechanisms prompted their disparaging behavior. They began recovering what they lost.

Many couples are successful as a team because they stopped fighting amongst themselves. Instead, they live with the knowledge that they complement each other and can support each other in recapturing the parts of themselves they lost. It helps to make them great parents, wonderful individuals, and more successful in their professions. We, too, were only able to write this book because we operate as a team and put our diverse talents in the service of a common cause.

What It Was Really About

The scene at the beginning of the chapter describes how two people with different ideas about a vacation can still enjoy the trip. The contrasts are clear: Sabine wants a cultural vacation; Roland is pleading for a relaxing vacation.
Sabine says about her family: "My mother always said, 'What's in your head, no one can take away from you.' Even my grandmother appreciated the world of thinkers and education. In light of the global economic crisis she experienced, she knew that all material things could be lost—but not what you learned." In Sabine's family, at the very least you had to be a good student; nothing but a university degree and a doctorate would do. "But other things were neglected," Sabine explains. "Since my mother

anxiously watched over every step I took, I was rather lax when it came to doing things, to taking action." Sabine's core energy was exceptional as far as thinking was concerned, but at the expense of action.

With Roland, the exact opposite was true. In his family, hands-on was the maxim. When there was a problem, action was taken. When, after the war, the butcher shop wasn't doing well, Roland's father did something no one had done before: He packed a brick of hot meatloaf in his backpack and supplied Vienna's delis with it. That's how the business got going again. Look ahead, organize, and act was the motto. Studying wasn't a priority.

"My mother always said, 'Butchers don't need to know Latin.' So, I went to business school. 'You don't need to torture yourself like that,' was her opinion."

Roland was fascinated by Sabine's world of knowledge and culture. Up to that time, he had only known vacations by a lake, where you could go swimming and lie in the sun, but cultural activities weren't on the program.

"It's understandable that my parents looked for relaxation rather than spending hours walking through a city. They spent all year on their feet and didn't want an agenda during their free time."

With Sabine, the opposite was true. Her parents checked out all the sights on their vacations. Just strolling around without any particular goal was new for Sabine.

It's no coincidence that Sabine and Roland fell in love. Both were looking for a partner who possessed those particular elements of core energy that were limited in themselves. In the face of such contrasts, some couples begin to defend their own world. Sabine and Roland could have said: "My way of spending a vacation is the better one." Luckily they didn't, which enabled both of them to develop further.

Now they can each appreciate what the other contributes to the relationship, thereby creating a balance. They've also learned from each other: Roland now reads reference books, because he has a thirst for knowledge; he has expanded the thinking part of his core energy. Sabine, on the other hand, has become better at taking action; she is able to implement the knowledge she continually acquires, and even organizes conferences.

What You Can Do

🌱 Collect as many restrictive parenting maxims as possible. Then assign them according to the four areas of core energy. We've collected a few tenets to inspire you:

Maxims that restrict the area of "thinking":
- Leave thinking to the horses. They have a bigger head.
- I'll explain that when you're older.
- You and your ideas. Stop dreaming.
- We don't talk about such things.
- Thinking about it doesn't get the job done.

Maxims that restrict the area of "feeling":
- You don't have to be afraid.
- A brave man feels no pain.
- Go to your room, you sourpuss.
- High spirits are seldom a good thing.

- Don't rejoice too soon or you'll have bad luck.
- I'll slap your face, so you'll have a reason to cry.
- Aren't you ashamed of yourself?
- Pride comes before a fall.

Maxims that restrict the area of "acting":
- Don't climb up there or you'll fall.
- Can't you sit still for a moment?
- Let me do that. I'm better at it.
- Playing doctor is not allowed in our family.
- That's too dangerous for girls.

Maxims that restrict the area of "feeling":
- This sweater isn't itchy.
- You don't need your hands for looking.
- Don't touch that. It's not for small children.
- Don't stare at people like that.
- This is not for your ears.
- Eat what's on your plate.
- Don't put that in your mouth.
- Don't stick your nose into things.
- Give your aunt a kiss. She doesn't smell bad.

🌱 Which area was most restricted? And which of the other three was most pronounced?

🌱 Make a list of the characteristics that annoy, irritate, or anger you most in your partner, and that you might catch yourself restricting in them.

🌱 Make a list of characteristics and behavior you especially admired in your partner during the initial infatuation phase. Of the four areas—thinking, feeling, acting, sensing—which of these were especially fascinating?

🌱 Go on a journey of discovery with your partner to uncover special skills. Then agree on a time period, for example, one or two weeks, in which you show your mutual appreciation once a day. For example: "It's great how you think about a project and contemplate each step carefully before you carry it out." Or: "I love the way you show your feelings, for example, how happy you are when you get a present."

🌱 Remember the example of Veronica, Werner, and the snowfield from the beginning of the chapter? Invite your partner to do something which you haven't done for a long time, or have never done together. Start with small steps. If your partner is afraid of heights, don't start with a high mountain, but take a hike over some hills. Invite your partner to try out something new with the motto: "Even if your heart starts pounding, it's your life, and it's good to try something new and re-discover all of your core energy."

4. The Dynamic Duo

The Turtle and the Hailstorm

"Hey, Sabine, didn't we agree that the kids should watch less TV? Why is Florian watching right now? This program really isn't for children."

"Kids also have to relax, Roland. Just let him."

"What do you mean by 'relax'? I think you're talking about yourself. You're the one who wants to relax."

Roland goes on, getting louder and louder: "I'm so sick of it! We decide on something, and you don't stick to it."

Sabine is silent.

"Well, you're not saying anything! That means you agree with me!"

"Not at all," Sabine answers, and continues putting on makeup, which Roland had interrupted.

"Hey, I'm talking to you!"

"I don't answer anyone talking to me in that tone."

Roland's anger increases. "I just don't get it! We agreed that the kids could watch just one show a day, and now you ignore it!"

Sabine remains silent, and Roland becomes more and more enraged.

"Say something! Talk to me! Whenever we have a conflict, you clam up!"

"Oh, just leave me alone."

Finally, Roland loses his composure. "That's exactly what I mean," he shouts. "Whenever we should be talking, you clam up. Come on, say something!"

Sabine remains silent. After a while: "I know you're right. I was wrong again. It's always the same with me ..."
"And now that submissive jabber!" Roland screams, totally beside himself. "I've had it. I've had enough. I'm leaving!" With that, he slams the apartment door behind him.

Minimizers and Maximizers—Two Opposite Temperaments

Stressful situations are not easy to handle. We get into a whirlwind in which we find it hard to control our actions. Instead, the autopilot takes over and reveals our basic temperament. In Imago, we speak of two temperaments: the minimizer and the maximizer. One withdraws inward, the other is extroverted, loud, and clear. We lovingly call these two types the Turtle and the Hailstorm.

The Turtle

What does a turtle do when it's in danger? It retracts its head and feet as far as possible under its shell to protect itself. People with the basic temperament of a minimizer will act similarly: when they are scared, they withdraw, fall silent, freeze, or submit. Their energy is internalized. Like the turtle shell, this makes them feel secure, inaccessible.

Based on our experience, approximately two-thirds of people with this temperament are men; one-third are women. Someone can be a minimizer in a relationship, but a maximizer at their job. Which means that a person might be an extrovert, but becomes a minimizer during stressful and frightening situations in the relationship.

Freezing when in danger is a phenomenon in the animal world as well. It's an instinct, a survival strategy. A rabbit, for example, freezes at the sight of a snake, minimizing its breathing and heart rate. Submission is also practiced in the animal kingdom: a wolf that loses a fight lies on its back and exposes its throat.

With people, minimizing is an instinct as well. It happens automatically. It enables us to react to stress quickly and, ultimately, in a life-sustaining manner.

From the outside, the Turtle is often seen as being respectful. "Look at that couple! He rants and raves, and she stays calm." Or: "Can you believe that this man already admitted three times that he behaved badly, and his wife is still reproaching him." That's how the Turtle is perceived: as understanding, maybe even as the poor person who is oppressed by their partner.

Whether we consider a person with turtle behavior positive or rather annoying depends on which type we are and how we judge ourselves. If we mind being a Turtle, we'll confront the other Turtle: "Come on, say something!" Or if we identify with it, we say: "If someone talked to me like that, I'd also keep quiet."

Turtle behavior has advantages and disadvantages. An advantage is that the Turtle calms a storm by holding back and gives you the chance to think things over before doing anything rash. On the other hand, the Turtle makes it hard for the other person to make contact. It often brings communication to a standstill, hampering a constructive exchange.

The Hailstorm

A hailstorm is aggravating. It whistles around the corner and rattles everything that isn't tied down. It hurls hailstones into your face, and finally, it disappears as quickly as it came. The person we call a maximizer acts similarly. When he is afraid, he either becomes aggressive or flees, or does both in sequence. His energy is directed outwards, following the motto: attack is the best form of defense.

Even though the Hailstorm seems masculine, approximately two thirds of Hailstorms are women, about a third are men. And the same thing applies here: A person can be a Hailstorm in one situation, and in another—at work, for example—be somewhat withdrawn and introverted.

As with the minimizer, Hailstorms are all about one quick, unconscious reaction: attack or flee. It's the same with wildlife: when a tiger is threatened, it attacks. A zebra, on the other hand, survives by fleeing as quickly as possible.

Hailstorms are more readily perceived by others because they're easier to recognize than turtles. Our opinions on Hailstorms depend on what type we are and how we judge ourselves: "Look at that woman. She's screaming at the top of her lungs. No wonder he keeps quiet. He can't get a word in edgewise." Or, "That would drive me crazy, too, if I never got an answer. I'd get just as loud."

A Hailstorm can have two contrary qualities. On the one hand, it's in no way gentle and might even cause suffering. And inundating someone with a barrage of words is certainly not conducive to conversation. On the other hand, it puts all of its available energy into the relationship, and has many impulses. Unfortunately, it's often too much.

The relationship dance

Imagine two Turtles in conflict with each other. What happens? Probably not much. Both withdraw into their armor, cutting off communication at the outset. A dance together is not in the cards. Two Turtles would probably never get past the infatuation phase. They'd starve to death halfway there. Two hailstorms would likewise have little chance of a shared future in the long-term—probably all hell would break loose after a short while.

Our experience shows that in relationships, there is almost always a Hailstorm and a Turtle, at least as a tendency. And that's good. That's the only way to achieve a dynamic conducive to a relationship. Even organizations and teams need minimizers and maximizers who complement each other. When one of them is pushing too hard to get something done, the other restrains a bit, adds an element of calm, and makes time for thinking things through. Something one of them might never mention, the other calls by name and ensures that action is taken. Ideally, there is a balance between minds.

Both Turtle and Hailstorm have more positive and less positive qualities. Neither is better or worse than the other, even if it sometimes seems as if that were the case. The Turtle who stoically suffers the Hailstorm's attack might appear to be a hero. On the other hand, torpor and submission cause the Hailstorm to feel uncontrolled and guilty. The Hailstorm can also be celebrated as a hero, because it brings conflicts to the forefront. However, its energy may also be destructive and might injure the Turtle, causing it to withdraw even further into its shell. We have to see the entire dynamic inherent in a couple's dance.

How do you turn into a turtle or a hailstorm?

Think about your parents or the people who raised you. Do you recognize their basic temperaments? We almost always experience mothers or fathers as Hailstorm or Turtle and adopt one of the two behaviors.

Simone belongs to the one-third of women whose behavior corresponds to a turtle. She told us that she is like her father in that way. In a dialogue with her partner, Paul, she recounted, how she suffered when her mother—an olympic Hailstorm—attacked her father. "I had the feeling Dad couldn't defend himself at all. And that's when I probably decided subconsciously to become like Dad, so that he won't be alone."

Raphaela, a skilled Hailstorm, told us that she resembles her mother as far as her temperament is concerned. Each day, Raphaela experienced how her mother, a true turbo-Hailstorm, desperately tried to reach her husband, who was extreme in distancing himself. But her despair was so great that she could only scream. Raphaela said, "I saw my mother so desperate that I swore to myself: I'll do everything I can to support her so that she's not so alone. That's probably when I decided to become a Hailstorm."

Karl, a typical Turtle, tells his wife, Gabi, in a dialogue, how much he loves his father, and at the same time how hurt he was that his father had so little time for him. The worst part was when he kept hearing his mother say: "Your father is a terrible person. He doesn't care about us, that's why he's not coming home." Carl was sure that his father wasn't a bad person. It's just that he had never learned from his parents what love and contact meant. "At that time, I thought, even though Mom badmouths him, I still love Dad and want to be just like him."

Leo told us that once, as a child, he became furious because he couldn't figure out his homework. He tore up his exercise book, which made his father so angry that he hit Leo. Today Leo is the classic Hailstorm. In a dialogue, he said: "At that time I decided, I will never be beaten again. That's why I attack when someone seems dangerous to me, and that might even be my wife."

There are many different reasons for becoming a Turtle or a Hailstorm. This behavior develops quite early and is often due to what we experienced with our parents, and whether we identify more with our fathers or our mothers. Sometimes there is such a thing as a family tradition in which all men for many generations become Turtles or all women Hailstorms.

Of course, not everything depends on how we are socialized. Along with our parents' genes, we also inherit a disposition, a basic temperament, and a body type. This disposition is either intensified or minimized through education and the environment. In a world where it's advantageous to be a Turtle, people with the innate disposition to be a Hailstorm might still become a Hailstorm, but either a moderate one, or a lively Turtle. People with an innately calm, relaxed temperament will certainly become the classic Turtles in such a world. The inverse is also true in a Hailstorm world.

So, developing into a particular type is complex. It's hard to say how your children will develop, even if you believe you already recognize typical characteristics of one or the other. Don't try to steer your children in a specific direction; just let it happen. Whichever type your child unconsciously decides to be, will be the right one.

I can find my counterpart anywhere

Earlier in the chapter, you learned that the dynamics between two poles make sense. That is probably the reason why we keep on meeting opposites.

Jasmin, a Hailstorm, told us in couples therapy that she wants to leave Julius because, "It's just no fun with a Turtle. There's no joy, no pleasure, no sex."

A few months later, she changed jobs. Her new boss was—a Turtle, a much more extreme one than Julius. "I can hardly believe it," she said. "I want to break up with Julius, this silent, submissive man, and what happens? I wind up with a boss who doesn't give me feedback, doesn't talk, and appeases me when I confront him. Now it's clear to me: I have to look at my love relationship in terms of this dynamic!"

The Real Issue

Elena had two miscarriages, both in the eighth week of pregnancy. Now she's pregnant again. After an examination at the gynecologist's, she meets her husband, Peter, for dinner. He tells her about his exhausting day at work. Elena is disappointed that he doesn't ask her how the examination went, especially since it's been so difficult for them to have a child.

For a while, she tries to hide her disappointment, but then she explodes, and in her typical Hailstorm manner, she asks: "So, my doctor's appointment doesn't interest you at all, I guess?" Peter is startled because he had forgotten and remains silent at first, but then, during the ensuing quarrel, he tells her how sorry he was. Peter's gestures of submission anger her even more, and she bombards him with accusations. Peter remains silent. When they resume bickering, it's only about further allegations: "You never say anything," she complains. "You're so aggressive!" is his critique. But the real issue—the problem of the lost pregnancies—never enters the conversation.

The Goal

To keep this relationship dance from spiraling downward, you need to find a way to verbalize the actual issue. A first step is to recognize your own stress pattern. Are you a Hailstorm or a Turtle? The goal is to learn to approach each other. As a Hailstorm, you could, for example, learn not to blurt everything out, but take the time to relax a little first. As a Turtle, you could learn to communicate with your partner instead of clamming up.

It is important for every couple to be familiar with the principle of the minimizer and the maximizer. Many conflicts arise because one withdraws, and the other one lets loose. At the same time, it's precisely this dynamic that enhances a relationship. Two temperaments can be used together to overcome hurdles and reach common goals.

To assist you in mastering this couple's dance, the following procedure is very helpful:

1. Be self-aware: By becoming aware of which type you are, you can better recognize and understand your behavior.
2. Appreciate your own species: You can only change your own behavior if you appreciate it.

3. Appreciate the other species. It's just as important to value your partner for being different. That's not easy during a conflict, of course, but it can work in moments of security and closeness. A Turtle is valuable because it is patient, persistent, and can wait. The energy of the Hailstorm is important because it effects change and brings fresh air into the relationship.
4. Balance the energies. As a couple, you are most effective if the Turtle learns to come out of itself and the Hailstorm learns to contain its energy. It's not an easy path, but it's undoubtedly the most efficient in the long run. The alternative is to look for someone else. But chances are rather good that you'll wind up with a similar counterpart!
5. Remember that involuntary actions happen faster than voluntary ones. We need to be conscious of the fact that part of the human brain reacts spontaneously and instinctively, just like animals. We walk upright, can build skyscrapers and computers, send rockets to Mars, and come up with great ideas and visions. Still, there are situations where our ancient brain controls us by shutting off our intellect. In a stressful situation, a Hailstorm might accuse his beloved partner of things he would never say otherwise, of which he's ashamed later on. The involuntary reflex acts faster than the intellect, which makes you unaware that exploding isn't appropriate.

Let us always be aware that in moments of danger, we react with a specific stress behavior. When we feel stress and danger, we become extremely insecure. So, the goal of a relationship has to be to increase the level of security by making contact, lending an ear to each other, and being empathic and understanding. And in the case of a stressful situation, we can only change behavior by being aware of it and reflecting on the reason for it. Then we can react more suitably next time.

What It Was Really About

Sabine and Roland's temperaments are easily assigned. Sabine is the Turtle, Roland the Hailstorm.
"I developed into a turtle," Sabine comments, "with a turbo-Hailstorm as a mother, and a turbo-Turtle as a father. My older brother Thomas decided, subconsciously of course, to be a Hailstorm, and I often watched him ranting and raving with my mother, even up to the point of physical violence." Sabine decided to become a Turtle because the scenes between Thomas and their mother frightened her.
"Maybe it was also, in part, loyalty towards my father that I became a Turtle. I saw him as someone who clumsily tried to be a good husband, but was constantly devalued by her. To be close to him, and because 50 percent of my genes are from him, I always saw him as a role model."
"I was often home alone," Roland recounts, "and in school, I felt lonely and excluded by my classmates, too. I remember our class representative always taking center stage. Probably at some point, I decided to be just as strong and to fight. I also wanted to be one of the first ones chosen for the soccer team."
Roland's mother was a Turtle, his father, a Hailstorm. His father

was extroverted and good at making contact with people, while his mother remained in the background. "My mother always said that behind every successful man, there's a successful woman. I often wished that she would take herself more seriously. I knew right from the beginning: Being energetic is more attractive and desirable. I decided to become a Hailstorm."

The scene at the beginning of the chapter makes it clear that the conversation was initially about TV and how to approach agreements. But in the course of the discussion, they lost the topic. Now it was all about Roland getting louder and Sabine falling silent. When her silence wasn't successful, she changed to submission. That infuriated Roland even more, and when he couldn't get a grip on his emotions, he fled.

For Sabine and Roland, it was necessary to separate the "how" from the "what." For one thing, they should have made a tenable agreement about the subject of TV. For another, they had to become aware of their basic temperaments and find a way to get along better. Roland had to accept the fact that his Hailstorm behavior forced Sabine to withdraw even more into her shell. Sabine had to understand that subservience makes her smaller than she is. If she wanted to present herself to the full extent of her abilities, she had to learn to engage in confrontations.

What You Can Do

🌱 Are you a Turtle or a Hailstorm? How do you react, for example, if you're hunting for the last gifts on Christmas Eve and someone bumps into you on the street? Do you push back like a Hailstorm? Or do you yield like a Turtle? Let your partner know which type you are.

🌱 Take a look at your family: who was a Turtle and who was a Hailstorm? Who was more or less respected? Who did you identify with or take as a role model?

🌱 What's your greatest fear when turning into a Turtle or a Hailstorm? Make notes about this. Reflect on what sets off stress and anxiety in you. Make a ranking. Which fear is the greatest, which is the least?

🌱 What do you need from your partner to feel secure? Make a list with ten items in ascending order and compare notes. Reflect on your own needs and let your partner talk about theirs. Thank them for their willingness to share.

🌱 What do you admire in your partner for being a Turtle or a Hailstorm? Write down ten reasons. For each of the next three days, write one of those reasons on a post-it and stick it in a spot where your partner is sure to see it; the bathroom mirror, for example. "Dear Hailstorm, I admire you for getting so much done." Or: "Dear Turtle, I appreciate your patience."

5. An Honest Look at Yourself Before Presenting Your Partner with a Relationship Book

A chapter especially for her

Sabine's friend Karin says, "Listen, Sabine, I don't want to worry you, but don't you find it strange that Roland just interrupted his vacation, supposedly so he wouldn't miss his therapy group?"

"Yes, it seems strange to me, too," Sabine answers, and looks at her friend, grief-stricken. "Do you think he's with someone else, too?"

When Roland returns two days later, two enraged women confront him.

"I agreed to join that group. Besides, I had to take care of something for the company."

Roland tries to defend himself, but Sabine and Karin are persistent.

"Do you think we're stupid? You're having an affair with another woman. Why don't you admit it?"

At first, Roland is shocked, but then—then he admits it. "Yes, I admit it. There's another woman in my life."

Now, it's Sabine's turn to be afraid. "W-what?" she stammers. And then after a while, "Now I understand why you won't read the relationship book I gave you. You'd rather take up with another woman than work out our problems."

Roland looks concerned. He feels quite uncomfortable and tries to calm her.

"I was so hoping that you'd be different than my father," Sabine continues. "My mother was right. You can't depend on men!"
"Do you really think that helps us now?"
"It helps me. My mother was skeptical of you right from the beginning. 'Take a good look at who you're getting involved with,' she said. I should have looked for the right mix between my brothers. That's not you! They always had time for me. Not something you can claim."
"Great! That's just what I need right now. You're constantly comparing me to your brothers and your father! I might as well go back home."
"Good idea! Get out. I never want to see you again!"

There's a lot that can be said about what shapes women, how they act, and why they are the way they are. The same holds true for men. However, in this chapter we will take a look at some aspects of being a woman and make some proposals. It should help you to become aware of what you're all about, how to better get along with yourself and your partner. It would also make sense for you to read the following chapter for "him"— not to find ways to criticize, but to get to know a new perspective.

It's always me working on the relationship

A look at our therapeutic practice clearly shows: It's always the women who want to "drag" their men to therapy. Maria was one of them. She called our assistant and said: "I'm interested in couples therapy, but my husband definitely won't want to come." Fortunately, we hold regular introductory evenings in which anyone can participate, anonymously and without obligation. Thus, both Maria and Jason came.

After the lecture, we started talking. Jason found our information very interesting. "I don't think much about these things. My wife knows a lot more about psychology and gave me some books to read. But to be honest, I leave them lying around on the bedside table. For my wife's sake, though, I would come to a workshop like this." Maria sighed. "What should I do with a man who does it for my sake rather than out of his own interest?"

Let's be honest to ourselves, dear women. Of course you want to do something for your relationship, and couples therapy would be great, but at the same time, isn't it sometimes the easier way out to hide behind your partner's "no"? We're quite often ambivalent, and even a little relieved, when we can depend on the fact that our partner is against it.

It's nice to see yourself in the active role, however, if your partner agrees, things might look a little different to you. As soon as he says: "Okay, let's go ahead with it," your fears and concerns surface. But then it's hard to back out!

It makes a big difference whether you discuss relationship problems with your best friend or in individual therapy, or with your partner at a couples therapist. You can tell your friend all kinds of things, and she'll sympathize with you. But if your partner is sitting across from you, and you're explaining all your wishes and desires, your wording will be different, knowing your partner won't see everything your way. He'll also present his fears and frustrating experiences, and you'll have to learn to deal with it. And after the session, you'll be going home with this man, and the session will have an ongoing effect. It's undoubtedly easier talking with a friend.

All women who confront their partners with couples therapy, thus initiating a process of development, deserve the greatest appreciation. The same, of course, is true for all men who take the initiative. At the same time, even hesitating men deserve our gratitude. As the initiator, you can use this delay to clear up your ambivalence one hundred percent. You'll be amazed by the effect it can have. Even if at the end he only agrees as a favor to you, take his willingness as a gift, because it's totally enough for a start.

I had a difficult childhood

To shape the relationship with our partner to our satisfaction, it's necessary to be aware of our origins. The same holds true for men. However, it's not enough to shed light on the past. We draw strength by accepting what was, and letting go of constraints and making peace with our ancestors. Then we have the chance for a clearer view of our future.

Appreciation and gratitude toward your mother and grandmother are the basis on which you can build your life and your relationship. Our female ancestors in particular can give us so much strength! Being appreciative and grateful seems easy for some, but not for others, who have a bitter aftertaste because they experienced a lot of pain in their childhoods. And for many, it's certainly not an easy process coming to terms with childhood hurts, fears, and frustrations.

What if your gratitude toward your mother or grandmother is only superficial or indirect? You run the risk of unconsciously copying your mother's life. You adopt behavior patterns that aren't at all right for you. Your mother grew up in a totally different time with different problems. She might have experienced war, and overcome hunger and poverty—her ultimate goal was to survive, and that's what influenced her actions. As her daughter, you live in a different time and are confronted with different fears and hardships. That is why it's crucial to verify whether the behavior you learned from your parents is beneficial for your own life and goals.

If you have a hard time being thankful toward your parental home, remember that your parents passed on what they could. If you missed your mother's affection, it might be that she had no chance to learn how to be loving from her own mother. If your self-esteem could not grow because of your mother's constant criticism, her actions might have resulted from having experienced the same reprimands herself.

Even if you live the opposite of what you learned from your mother, you're not free. It only seems like it. Your ancestors influence your behavior as well—for instance, if you are living contrary to a relative's life and not according to your own nature or the right way of life for you. If you're able to come to terms with your past, appreciate and be grateful to your mother and grandmother, it will be easier to develop self-love and shape your life and your relationship according to your own standards.

My husband doesn't help with the housework

Emancipation or not, women are caught between work, family, and partnership—all very demanding. It is still socially accepted that the man's focus is primarily on his profession, and the woman is responsible for the children. In our practice, we often hear of women's great desire for equality and appreciation for their efforts as women, mothers, and professionals.

"You never take care of the kids," is a possible reproach. But reproaches rarely achieve the hoped-for results. If you want to build equality between you and your partner, say goodbye to the recriminations. Include him in family life. Instead of: "You never help with the housework," ask him next time to do the vacuuming. And—just as important—trust him to do it right, even if it's not as perfect as you expect.

In this context, learn from the role models of previous generations: to what extent are you really free to take your own, emancipated path? We often cling to the values of our mothers and grandmothers, and find it hard to bear knowing that they wouldn't approve of our husband tending to the kids while we go out to eat with a friend.

Who is better – him or me?

Many women are in constant conflict with their partners. For example, if he's successful in his profession, she wants to show that she's as least as good as he. The reason is often that the man lives what the woman can't allow herself. Or she won't admit to having that specific competence.

Nina and Kurt are a successful, modern couple. They both have the same profession. When they came to our practice, Nina complained that her husband was much better at asserting himself than she. He was better at negotiating and better at implementing his ideas. That often put her in a bad mood. When she came home in the evening, tired, she often provoked an argument about it. Instead of saying how unhappy she was, she criticized Kurt for his lack of support with the housework.

Later, after a few counseling sessions, Nina understood that her reproaches stemmed from the fact that she could be certain she was more competent in the household than he was. Kurt's compliments—he considered her much more competent in her job—went unheard.

In therapy, we suggested that Nina accepted her husband as her ally and not as a competitor. In the dialogue that followed, the roots of Nina's sense of inferiority came to light. When Nina was a child, she regularly saw her mother favoring her brother. If he did something well, he was praised. Her own good grades from school were taken for granted. The message for Nina was clear: Men can do things better. She learned something else from her mother: men have to be criticized and devalued. Because Nina's mother liked to grumble about men, "who have it much easier in life."

On the other hand, Kurt realized that he hadn't given his wife enough support. In several dialogues, they found a new way: On the day before her next customer meeting, Nina should go through her presentation with Kurt. But contrary to Nina's expectations, Kurt couldn't add anything to her preparations—she was that good. Because of this support, the presentation was a huge success.

It's much more effective for women to see their partners as allies than to compete with them. This also allows them to ask for support and better develop their own strengths.

I'm not pretty enough

Women are much less satisfied with their bodies than men are. They're constantly criticizing something: my nose is too big, my hair too straight, my breasts too small, my thighs too large, my toes crooked, my pubic hair badly shaven. Interesting, however, is that most men find the bodies of their wives not only "just right" but very attractive. Quite often, men even find the body parts their wives criticize in themselves exceptionally beautiful. Yes, dear women, that's a fact!

Why are women so strict with themselves and with each other, and much milder with the physical inadequacies of their partners? Although they compliment their husbands less often than the other way around, they rarely mention things that bother them. Again and again, during couples therapy, we hear a man say: "You've never told me that it bothers you that I'm in such bad shape."

Concerning breast enlargement, labia corrections, and other self-mutilation, it saddens us that women often have such a poor relationship with their bodies. Plastic surgeries are expensive and usually don't have the hoped-for effect. Fewer wrinkles surely won't increase the love of a partner, and labia correction usually doesn't have an effect on sex life.

Of course, it's always good to take care of your body. Stay active, eat healthily, and pamper it every now and then. Be gentle and loving to your body. Accept it with all its distinctive characteristics. And, in spite of its supposed blemishes, be thankful that it carries you through life.

Sexual assault

Unfortunately, many women have experienced physical assaults. Especially with adolescent girls, this is a highly sensitive topic, so that even experiences that seem insignificant may have adverse effects. Just the idea of a father's fantasy that the daughter would be a better wife than the mother could be disturbing. That's emotional abuse, and even if there is no physical force, it's bad enough. The misty-eyed look of a dreaming father or a seemingly harmless touch on the shoulder may be enough to disturb a daughter emotionally. And in the worst case, it ends in sexual abuse.

Please tell your partner these stories and about the pain you feel. Ask him to take your pain seriously and hold you in his arms, when emotions and tears overwhelm you. If you don't feel secure enough, get help through therapy. Pain healed in such a way can generate a more intense security and intimacy than one might possibly imagine.

Women often suppress such abuse. It appears in dreams or during sex, and often, neither the woman nor her partner knows how to deal with them. Whatever reaction she has, the man could presume he's the cause, and distance himself as a result. How could he know the actual reason behind it all? If you don't talk about these things with him, all he can do is misinterpret your bad mood.

Just as important is communicating your desires and wishes concerning intimacy. However, should your husband find out that you've experienced sexual abuse, he'll feel insecure because he doesn't want to hurt you. Therefore, he needs your guidance. It's equally important for both of you to understand the difference between childhood abuse and adult sexuality. As a child, one is at someone's mercy, helpless, full of shame, and perhaps even feelings of guilt. As far as sex with a partner goes, a grown woman can decide for herself, participate, and be passionate. Then she isn't a victim, but a conscious designer of strength, power, and devotion. It's all about discovering and respecting each other's limitations and nurturing each other's desires and yearnings.

He only ever wants one thing

Women need dialogue to feel intimacy, and then sexuality and physical contact are possible. Very few women wouldn't agree with that. But do you, as a woman, know what men need to feel secure and intimate? Yes, it's a fact: men need physical contact. It doesn't mean having sex; often it's enough, for example, to greet each other with physical contact.

Men sometimes shy away from being greeted with a hug because they're in a bad mood or upset about something or other. But if you put your arms around his waist, it gives the feeling of intimacy, and makes it easier for him to ask: "How was your day?" It doesn't mean that you have to put up with his moods. Nobody should have to twist themselves around to do something they genuinely don't want to. What we are trying to say is: accept that men are made different, when it comes to establishing security and closeness.

The reason men often need direct, explicit, physical contact is that they have little physical contact during their daily routine. Women have it better: they hug their girlfriends, their parents, and their children—this is simply less common with men. This also creates the unconditional desire for sex, which women then shrug off, as: "He only ever wants one thing." In truth, he generally needs more physical contact in everyday life, and you can supply that. Hold hands when you go for a walk, pull his arm around your waist, or touch his knee under the table when you're having dinner with friends.

Men want to make us happy

For most men, there's nothing better than having a partner who is happy, content, and passionate. Studies have underscored this fact. There is only one problem: they often don't know how to go about it. In one of our couples workshops, one of the men summed it up. He said: "I'd like a plan of action."

Do you know Woody Allen's film, *Everything You Always Wanted to Know About Sex* (*but were afraid to ask)*? In that film, an Italian man desperately tries to satisfy his wife and does everything according to an instruction manual. In the end, he's successful, thankfully! But before you give your partner a book, why don't you tell him about your needs and desires—not just in bed, but in general.

Don't expect him to already know what makes you happy. Such guessing games might lead in a very different direction. As a woman, you don't always know what makes him happy and what he desires, either. Men like having a plan of action, so please him— and yourself at the same time.

What It Was Really About

It's terrible finding out that your partner has another woman. Up to that moment, Sabine and Roland had gone through numerous power struggles. They had just successfully gotten through that phase—but Sabine had forgotten to pay attention to being a woman. Roland had been suffering in the relationship because there was no joy, no fun, and little intimacy.

Instead, Roland was given relationship guides. "I'm not satisfied with you as a man," is one message behind such a present. "Do something about it!" Sabine had been influenced by her mother's opinion of men: You can't depend on a man.

"There were several ideal men in my family—for instance, my mother's father. He was a tall and strong man. His wife, a Jewish woman, had been devastated by the Holocaust, and she left my mother alone much of the time. But her father was there and took on something like the mother-role.

When my parents met, my father couldn't satisfy my grandfather's strict ideals. He wasn't good enough. They married anyway, or maybe precisely because of that, and things unfolded as they were bound to: They engaged in power struggles, and instead of confronting his wife, my father had an affair. Since that time, my mother was a living example for me: 'You cannot rely on men.'"

Sabine's brothers were the next idealized figures. "The men in my mother's life were measured by the standards of my grandfather's and my two brothers. So, I did that too, unconsciously. And Roland couldn't measure up to that standard. So, I gave him relationship guides because I didn't know how else to deal with it. I wanted Roland to measure up to my ideal."

Roland's affair was a wake-up call for Sabine. She became aware of the fact that she had to reconsider her image of men instead of hurtfully withdrawing. The same is true of her image of women.

"I began thinking about what was wrong with me and started to criticize my body. Roland's girlfriend must surely be more desirable. But my friend, Karin, opened my eyes. She said: 'You're a wonderful woman, and Roland is lucky to have you. Only in some things you have become lackadaisical, and you know it!' That opened my eyes. My criticism about my body was because of the image of women my mother had communicated to me. Once she even dyed her brunette hair blond to compete with the other woman in my father's life."

In spite of Sabine's hurt feelings, she made an important decision: She was willing to take a good look at the situation. She wanted to find out the reason there had been room for another woman in her relationship. "What does Roland have with that woman that he can't have with me?" That was the crucial question.

Roland also didn't have a real role model to show him how to confront a partner who withdraws and gives up being a woman. "It's not enough to give me a relationship guide," he told her when they decided to reassess their relationship. "I need you as a woman. I know how much I hurt you. Had I known what was going on inside me, I would have confronted you differently. Please forgive me." Together they discovered what was missing in their relationship: recognizing where they both needed to evolve in order to share a future.

What You Can Do

🌱 What role models did your mother impart on you? What ideal of partnership did your parents convey? What did your mother teach you about how to treat a man? Reflect on the effect on you of the preconceptions of your female ancestors. Based on your family structure and tradition, what is forbidden to experience with a man? What is especially valued? What did your mother teach you about sexuality in general?

🌱 Discover your body. Stand in front of the mirror naked, and find the things you like. Be grateful for your beautiful breasts, your belly, and your legs. Thank your body for carrying you through life.

🌱 Notice how you greet your partner and try out new ways of greeting him, especially regarding physical contact to express your love (not just sex).

🌱 Get to know your own needs. Make a list of things you no longer want in the relationship, and another with things that you want. Positively phrase the latter. Instead of writing: "I don't want you to pinch my butt," formulate it positively: "Please, if you want to touch me, do it firmly and clearly."
Try to talk to your partner about such things. Let him know what you would like done differently or introduced into your relationship. Begin the conversation with a statement of appreciation.

🌱 Make a list about what you'd like from your partner in terms of appreciation, love, and recognition. On a scale of 1 to 5 (1 is easy, 5 especially hard) assess how well you can accept that love. Wherever it's difficult for you, make a plan for how you could succeed in being better able to accept this love and appreciation.

🌱 What excuses do you make to avoid talking with your partner? What could be a first step in finding a more direct form of communication? (See also Chapter 7.) If you catch yourself complaining about your partner to your close friend, try to talk about yourself instead. Your friend's solidarity helps temporarily and only to a degree; in the long term it doesn't help your relationship to grow or renew. Do you sometimes think about other men and fantasize? Why do you have those fantasies? Could you experience them with your partner?

6. Discover Your Feelings for Your Own Sake; Your Wife Will Be Thankful

A chapter especially for men

"Have you made an appointment with a therapist? A few weeks ago, you said you would start therapy."
"You and your therapy! Why don't you go to a shrink! You're the neurotic one, don't bother me with it."
"Roland, just yesterday you told me that you feel very overwhelmed. You had tears in your eyes and asked yourself if this is really your calling."
"Did I say that? I don't remember."
"Darling, that was just yesterday. I love you much too much to watch you carry that huge load on your shoulders. Therapy would lighten things up for you."
"All they do is talk things to death and stir up the past. I believe in letting the past rest in peace."
"I don't agree with you. The future needs an origin. If you're looking for answers about your future, you can find them in therapy, and in the process, you'll certainly take a look at your past."
"Besides, I don't have time for it. I have to implement the new distribution system in the company, that's much more important."
"You are important, Roland. Don't do it for me. Do it for yourself."
"By the way, did I mention what my new primary doctor said? I told him I want to take a speaking course because I always feel

so insecure when I have to speak in front of a group. He also said that I should go to therapy. He gave me a folder; maybe I'll set it up."

"Oh, sure, if some so-called expert suggests therapy, that's something totally different than when I suggest it."

It would be presumptuous to state that typical male behavior could be described in a single chapter. Besides, all men can't be lumped together; after all, each person is an individual. Still, in this chapter we would like to focus on some aspects we encounter again and again in our practice. We're going to shed some light on them, and give suggestions on how to better handle certain situations.

We invite you, dear reader, to read the previous chapter for women; not to give you more material to badmouth women at your next meeting with the guys, but to gain another point of view and look at the world through a different lens.

This endless emotionalism

Take an honest, critical look at your life. Is your relationship the way you had always hoped it would be? When was the last time you asked yourself what you contribute to preventing it from being the way you want it to be?

Unfortunately, most men have never learned to confront themselves with such questions or to express their feelings. "A brave man feels no pain," is the motto of most men, with which they keep their emotions hidden. When they don't pause to reflect, they deprive themselves of consciously experiencing how life is being lived. "Speech is silver, silence is golden," is another belief with which many men suppress their feelings.

Others are fortunate to have absorbed feminine values, but then they might be missing the strong, masculine side. A man in couples therapy once said: "I used to be macho. My wife wasn't happy with that, and ultimately, neither was I. Now I'm a softie, but that doesn't satisfy her either. I'm confused."

We can only fulfill our hopes and expectations by taking a close look at them beforehand. Dear men, if you want to be more satisfied, dare to look at what really matters. You can find that out by genuinely getting to know yourself. You can do yourself a great favor by getting in touch with your feelings and acknowledge your history that made you who you are today.

It doesn't help anyone to belittle feelings or sweep them under the carpet. That only bypasses our core. Grappling with one's history—childhood and all the wonderful and even problematic memories—allows us to live our lives authentically, intensively, and with self-determination. It's not only possible, but also desirable, to adopt some behaviors from women, because for the most part, they have learned to deal with emotions. Ask your partner to support you—that would be an excellent first step.

Like father, like son?

Our male ancestors are our role models on which we orient ourselves from an early age. That's often quite difficult, because those role models are either irritating or completely outdated. Or, our fathers were conspicuous in their absence, which in a way is also a role model, but not one worth emulating.

Some have the urge to copy their fathers, others want to be nothing like them, and strive for the opposite. The problem is, no matter whether you copy them or act as their opposites, it's probably not consistent with what you need. You're not your father's replica; you have your own personality, which is made up of a combination of your father, your mother, and your environment. Finally, you're living in a different time that confronts you with completely different challenges. Women have a different self-image, and the role of men within family and society has changed. At work, social skills have greater importance; children have more freedom.

In any case, it's worthwhile to design your own concept of manhood. Not everything you grew up with is good, nor is it all bad. To find out what's right for you, it helps to take a look at the men in your family and question: What did you take on subconsciously, as opposed to willingly? Which strengths did your ancestors exhibit that are inactive in you?

True male identity means that you choose what you wish to integrate into your life and what you don't. Hans, for example, told us that his father always yelled at his mother—and subconsciously he decided never to yell at his wife and always be loving. But he forgot to set boundaries. When there was a conflict, he withdrew. His wife, a true Hailstorm (see Chapter 4), wanted to reach Hans and feel his emotions, and she became more and more vehement. Then, one day, Hans yelled back at his wife—which frightened him, because now he had become like his father after all. He was ashamed of himself and then surprised that his wife was happy about his outburst, because finally she was able to feel his boundaries.

So, it's not enough to decide not to become like your father. Hans didn't want to be aggressive, but it was important for him to differentiate between aggression and firmness. Expressing his anger or conviction to his wife is only offensive when it's done in the wrong tone. But Hans hadn't quite figured that out. During couples therapy, he was able to define exactly which parts of his father he didn't want to take on, what he wanted to develop for himself instead. Together with his wife he learned to set boundaries, demonstrating his steadfastness without becoming aggressive.

I am doing it for my wife's sake

In our practice, we often hear: "I only came as a favor to my wife." Just as often, we hear the woman say: "If he's only doing it for me, I don't need it." The fact of the matter is: as men, we often need the woman to initiate. And regardless of the reason, we finally agreed to do something for the relationship—after all, it's a start! It's a proof of love that we agree to take on something new, something that might seem foreign, and men deserve some gratitude if they are willing to take such a step.

But many men want to delay that first step, and some never take it. Next time your partner asks you: "Will you do it for me?" and your first impulse is to say "No," close your eyes before answering. Just think, there were probably many situations in your life where you wouldn't have hesitated to do your partner a favor. Maybe that was during the first phase of infatuation, when you were wooing her, maybe later. And now, when your relationship may be at a critical juncture, don't you want to do it for her?

At work, if a project was in trouble or about to fail, you'd definitely do your best to figure out the cause and find alternatives to make your project successful. If your partner asks you to go to couples therapy, it's basically the same thing. She wants to bring the relationship to a safe haven. So, if you don't want to go into therapy as a favor to her, do yourself a favor and find out where the problem lies. Get to know yourself better. Then, if your wife says: "See, I told you that therapy would do you good," don't take it as a reproach, but thank her for the impetus.

I will only accept help when the water is up to my neck

When Simon and Erika came to couples therapy, Erika told us that she had been trying for ten years to get him to come. Only now was he ready for therapy. The reason: Simon's doctor had diagnosed him with a serious illness. It suddenly struck him how right she was that he should do something good for himself. Now, in light of this severe illness, he had a different perspective on life. He was ready and willing to look into the problems of their relationship and take a closer look at his life.

Men in particular often need a crisis before they are willing to investigate their emotions. In many cases, they put it off until they hear words like, "I'm in love with someone else." Only then are they open and willing to take the "risk." For Simon, the bad medical diagnosis was not the end. With his wife's help and therapy, they were able to reconnect with one another. Simon recovered, and they reached a new, more profound connection in their relationship.

She spends hours talking about the same thing

Men like to have solutions at hand. You listen to a problem, and immediately you're thinking about how to solve it. It is often incomprehensible that women can talk about the same subject for hours on end, without formulating a solution.

Of course, women are also solution-oriented. But they also tend to "need a good cry" first. The greatest gift you can give your partner is to listen to her and be understanding. Talking relaxes most women. Then, when they feel valued and affirmed, they are ready to talk about solutions. Maybe then they find their own way, or gratefully consider your suggestions.

It takes some practice to hold back instead and just show understanding. The good thing about it is, the more you practice, the better you get. Just think about how strenuous it is, having to listen to your wife talks for hours on end. "My wife can talk for hours about feelings," men say. "I really can't listen anymore, so I just say, 'sure, sure.'" You could save yourself a lot of aggravation if you took the time to listen actively for ten minutes in the first place! Not only would it save time, but it would also create a deeper bond between the two of you.

My childhood was perfect!

Some men have the impression their wives only want to talk them into believing they had problems when they speak about their childhood. In those cases, men tend to defend their childhood: "I had the happiest childhood one could imagine. Please stop saying I had problems with my family!"

How do women get this idea? Do they want to hurt their partners? No. All they want is to help, but they are sometimes clumsy in the way they go about it. Essentially, women always want to encourage their men to find their true selves—to find their male identity so that they can commit themselves completely to the relationship.

Patricia's parents hurt and disparaged her. So, she watched very closely to see how Herman's parents treated him. There were definitely things that she disliked; in couples therapy, she went on the offensive with Herman immediately—and he consistently defended his parents instead of taking a closer look. For Herman, Patricia's attacks were just one more reason for him to avoid dealing with his childhood.

Eventually, though, he did, and it turned out that he had frequently felt belittled by his father. Herman's mother had been unhappy with her husband, so she gave all of her love on her children, and that made Herman think he had had a happy childhood. He had suppressed the pain he felt at his father's absence. When Herman stopped defending his childhood and was ready to deal with it more directly, then Patricia could relax, too. She stopped reproaching Herman and concentrated on her own history, because now she felt they were allies and equals.

My wife is so powerful

Saskia and Alexander came to us with a classic problem: Saskia was at home with the kids, alone with the daily chores. Alexander, totally entwined in his job, had little sense of family life. Saskia didn't feel appreciated, and in the evening, she said to him: "You keep coming home later and later, don't you want to come home anymore? Aren't you at all interested in my life?" Saskia, a self-assured, emancipated woman, remained faithful to her wish for a relationship, commitment, and togetherness, and voiced this thought unequivocally and directly. During therapy, Alexander told us: "My wife is so powerful. If I don't come home on time, I'm terrified."

Alexander forgot to call her at agreed times, came late to dates they had made, and danced with other women at a party. During therapy, he realized: "Now I understand that all those little acts were passive aggressive behaviors, but that was the only way I could defend myself against my wife. I felt confined, dominated, and patronized." During sessions, he wanted to get to the bottom of things.

Saskia was very grateful to him for joining her in therapy and helped him in his search for answers. Alexander had been a very sad little boy. His mother had been unhappy because shortly after his birth, his father had left the family. Little Alex felt his mother's grief, but at the same time he felt her dominance, because her motherly love sometimes went overboard and degenerated into surveillance. During a session, he said, "I think I was already angry then, when I saw how badly off my mother was. She was so in love with my father, and he hurt her so much. As her son, I couldn't disappoint her as well."

What Alex experienced as a child provided the foundation for the life of today's adult Alexander. He was furious with women because he couldn't live his life as he wanted to—not as a child, and not as an adult. He told Saskia: "Now I understand, when I come home late or miss a date we had, I disrespect your feelings and your achievements. But that was the only way I could compensate for the anger I felt towards my mother."

This is why it's so crucial that men become aware of the origin of their aggressions. On the surface, they do everything for the family, earn money to create a good life, but in the relationship, they lose touch with themselves and their partners. It's all about finding the source of their anger and aggression, and dispersing it. That doesn't mean maligning their mothers, who do their best, based on their own history.

They cannot pass the responsibility of their mothers onto their partners. They can only take it upon themselves to become aware of their own emotions. At its base, aggression is a good emotion: it shows there is energy present. Only, that energy must be applied sensibly, by being converted into a strength that serves the relationship.

Careful, this is a test

"Next time you're thinking of me, send me a message, okay?" Watch out, dear men, this is a test! Also: "If you really love me, you'll surprise me." Another test: "The way our relationship is going, I don't see any future. I want to split up." The problem is, men usually don't perceive those statements as tests. Because there is a fundamental question behind these statements: Are you committed to me? Will you stand by me, even in a crisis? Are you ready to fight for our relationship, even if I want to end it?

Iris and Gary came to us for an Imago couples workshop. Towards the end, there was an exercise in which we invited the couples to undertake a vision quest in their minds—a trip into the future. How should it look? Iris couldn't find any image and said to Gary: In my vision quest, I saw us separately if anything." Gary was flabbergasted, and said he didn't have a clear picture, either. "I knew it," Iris said. "We have no future together."

Two weeks later, they came and told us of their intention to separate. Together, they wanted to get to the bottom of the story. Both of their childhoods had been defined by being abandoned, so they both had a hard time envisioning a future as a couple. Neither of them had a clear vision, and they interpreted that accordingly. That's when Iris tested Gary, and he failed. She wanted him to fight for the relationship, but because of his own history, he didn't. Luckily, we were able to clear that up in their sessions so they had the chance to develop a shared vision.

Men test, too, but differently. If you come home late and your wife is still friendly and allows you your freedom, she has passed the test. If you tell her about a successful project that will get you a fat bonus at the end, and your wife is dismissive about it, she didn't pass the test. So, don't just get to the bottom of your wife's test, but of yours also.

What It Was Really About

When the conversation at the beginning of the chapter took place, Roland was busy defending his childhood. He grew up in an environment where it was considered good to feel emotions, but there was no room to express them. When Roland asked his mother about the war and his father's imprisonment, he was always told: "We don't talk about that. It's not good for Papa to talk about the war."

"But in the long run, it wasn't good for me to suppress my feelings. It was my primary doctor who ultimately made it clear to me that I had to do something about it and start therapy. Even though my wife had told me the same thing over and over again—that my family believed in authority—it was easier for me to accept the doctor's advice."

Roland grew up with five women: his mother, a nanny, and his three sisters. That undoubtedly helped him to develop a particular type of sensitivity. The therapy awakened his sensitive sides. Thus, he was able to bid the old patterns good-bye and begin a new family tradition where feelings are welcome.

What You Can Do

✦ When did you last tell your partner what you especially love about her? Make a list of ten things you could say to her, and for the following two weeks, communicate your appreciation every day. Also, think about how you can surprise your wife in the next few days or weeks (see also Chapter 10).

✦ Do you tend to defend your childhood? Then answer this question: who benefits from your defensiveness? You, your parents, your grandparents, your siblings, your wife? Ask a close friend next time you see him if he's had similar experiences.

✦ When was the last time you really listened to your wife? When was the last time you said: "Tell me about it,

I'll listen!" Invite your wife to chat with you and show her that you understand her. You might even consider mirroring her (see Chapter 1).

🌱 Has your wife suggested several times that you go to therapy together? If so, consider what actually stopped you. What are you afraid of? Talk about it. Thank her for trying to do something to help develop your relationship. Tell her why it's so hard for you to start therapy. Ask her to help find a way, which makes it acceptable for both of you.

🌱 Does your wife know about your secret wishes? Probably not, or they wouldn't be secret. Write down your strongest and most frequent visions and fantasies concerning your relationship and your sexuality. Don't just stick to one topic, sex for example. Try to write as long a list as possible, show it to your partner and discuss it.

🌱 Emancipate yourself. For example, you could take your child to the next doctor's visit. Tell your wife she can depend on your carrying out that task well—even if you go about it differently than she does.

7. A Thousand Reasons not to Talk to Each Other

Closeness can also be scary

"It's really mean of you to tell our friends how neglected I make you feel," Roland complains to Sabine on the way home after an evening with friends. "How can you complain about me to others? That's hurtful!"

"But that's the way it is: I feel totally neglected by you."

"I don't understand. Just yesterday I picked up your car from the tow lot after you called me all upset. Doesn't that mean anything?"

"So what? Besides, I didn't ask you to do it, and if that's what you're harping about now, I certainly don't need it."

"It's unbearable! I try to do my best, and then I'm accused of that, too!" Roland is furious—furious enough to fling his cell phone into the bushes. "On top of that, you act like you're so miserable and badmouth me in front of our friends!"

"I am miserable! You suppress me!"

Roland, in a rage, walks on, shoulders pulled up, fists stuck in his pockets. Sabine picks up Roland's phone and follows a few paces behind him on their way home.

The next day, both of them are quite busy with their jobs. When Sabine gets home, she calls Roland.

"I don't know when I'm coming home. I'm pretty busy," Roland tells her.

"But I'd like to talk about yesterday."

"I don't know when I'll be finished."

An hour later, Roland is still not home.

"When are you coming?" Sabine asks again on the phone.
"Well, somebody has to work. I'm still not done."
Another hour passes and Roland is still busy with his office work. When he finally gets home at 11 pm, Sabine is asleep.

The Space between You and Me

Have you experienced this as well? Your partner did something that's disagreeable to you. For example, he forgot Valentine's Day, and now your feelings are hurt. But instead of telling him directly how you feel, you complain to a close friend about him. And, while you're at it, you also tell her that you feel short-changed because he never helps around the house. Your friend sympathizes. She comforts you, and in the end you feel encouraged not to put up with all that anymore.

Did that solve your problem? Of course not! Your partner is still completely clueless and doesn't know how happy you would have been to get a bouquet from him. Perhaps in the meantime he realizes that he forgot and he feels guilty, but since you haven't said anything, he might think you don't mind.

In Imago Therapy, there is a term called couples interspace. It relates to what happens during contact between two people: the nature of the relationship, chemistry, and mood. It could happen, as in the above scene, that someone feels neglected or hurt. We then say that the couples' interspace has been polluted. There was an irritation, and now the harmony is disturbed. There's something in the air that needs clearing up. Maybe it was only a trifle: one partner's wrong word at the wrong time that irritated the other and caused them to withdraw and be less friendly than usual. The first partner reacts irritably or nags. They lose sight of love, appreciation, and mutual exchange.

Both bear responsibility

Both partners are equally responsible for dealing with irritations, injuries, desires, and wishes within the couples' interspace, not outside of it. For example, if it irritates you that your partner smacks his lips when eating, and you never mention it, then at some point that little thing turns into a big deal, and it can roll right over both of you—the typical snowball-effect.

It's easy to blame your partner for a problem, but that doesn't release you from blame for your irritable, immature behavior. Your partner is not the only one at fault for your frustration, just because he's the one smacking his lips while eating. That's only one side of the coin. If you don't raise the issue, then you are responsible for your frustration as well.

Guessing games, by the way, are quite popular, but they don't get you anywhere either. One partner withdraws, offended, deliberately clams up, and avoids looking at the other partner. After a few days, the first partner is more frustrated than ever because the second partner has failed to react. The only effective tool in such a situation is dialogue. There's no way around it, even if there seem to be many ways out.

Evasive Maneuvers

Every conflict, every irritation has a unique energy. There are different ways of managing this energy. Ideally, we gather our courage and seek a conversation. Then the energy flows constructively into the relationship. Often we swallow the anger, but then we lock up the energy inside ourselves. Most often, however, we look for a way out, an escape hatch, when the relationship frustration burns at our centers. Here, we have summarized the typical escape hatches—the different ways of avoiding confrontation and distracting from frustration—and divided them into three categories.

Escape hatches that can lead to disaster

Murder and suicide are the extreme ways out of the miseries of a relationship. It should never go that far. Within a relationship, there shouldn't ever be the threat of murder or suicide. "If you leave me, I'll kill myself," is undoubtedly the most severe threat we can make, but this cannot be a solution.

In our relationship, we threatened each other with the worst, too—but that was a long time ago. "Once I'm gone, you'll see how sorry you'll be," was the message we wanted to throw in each other's faces. Such statements are only made out of desperation—and the other one feels threatened. Today we know that, at that time, we weren't taking responsibility for our relationship. We didn't mention what hurt and irritated us; instead, we directed our energy destructively against ourselves and each other. Luckily, we didn't choose that escape hatch.

Escape hatches with serious consequences

Included among these escape hatches are separation, divorce, illness, addiction, and affairs. Chapter 8 describes the escape hatch called The Affair. You escape from conflicts into the arms of a third, loving person, and everything appears to be intact. Everything, that is, except the relationship that's actually at stake.

Of course, illness in itself is not a way out of a relationship; it's just a sickness that needs to be cured. But when this condition is used as a pretense not to talk about the actual issue, then it's an escape hatch.

"Look, I'm sick because you treat me like that," borders on blackmail. At the very least, it's an accusation that doesn't solve anything. Another escape hatch is when an illness is given more attention than necessary. "First, I have to take care of my health. We can talk when I'm well again."

Alcohol and drug addictions are often like a third person in the relationship. When you are drunk, you are no longer available for your partner and the conflict between you. That's what happened to Henry and Renata. They took on a massive project: to renovate a farm. Henry was responsible for the rough part of the work and was good at getting things done quickly. Renata was skilled and creative, full of persuasive ideas that not only appealed to her husband, but made her popular with a lot of other people as well. Henry felt more and more pushed into the background and was afraid he could not keep up with Renata.

He lacked the courage to talk to Renata about his fear and began spending the evenings drinking with a friend at a restaurant. It started to become a habit, and finally, an addiction. He needed the alcohol to drown his sense of inferiority. Renata felt rejected. She, too, had fears and would have liked to talk about them with Henry. But he was spending all his time with his other "love," alcohol. Before long, the subject of separation came up.

Separation and divorce are easily accessed escape hatches these days. On the one hand, it's a good thing that women no longer need to feel shackled in a marriage for purely financial reasons. On the other hand, it's unfortunate that divorce has become so quick and casual. It's fundamentally strange: In a company, each major decision is analyzed carefully. In love relationships, we prefer to escape the problematic arguments with the hope that the next relationship will be happier.

We're not saying that separation is not a solution. Sometimes it's actually the best way to go for both parties. But couples should take their time to find out what really is best for both of them. In approximately 95 percent of the couples we meet, separation is a way out rather than a conscious, mature, mutual decision.

Daily escape hatches

Immersing ourselves in work, taking care of the household, keeping the kids busy, engaging in club activities, playing sports, watching TV, etc.—to a reasonable degree, these are all useful and sensible activities. But they are also wonderfully convenient escape hatches to distract from relationship problems. Even individual therapy can be a way out. Of course, it's good to engage in self-development during a therapeutic process. But if talking with a therapist becomes a substitute for talking with a partner, it's a way out. In most cases, it makes more sense to include the partner in therapy. That's the only way both sides can become conscious of their responsibilities.

What makes all these escape hatches so attractive is that they are socially accepted. Occupying oneself caringly with kids or volunteering in a hiking club is most desirable. It's up to you to question yourself critically: Am I doing this in order to avoid talking with my partner? Am I escaping their accusations instead of facing the conflict?

Creating Awareness of Escape Hatches

How escape hatches are learned
The inner drive to find a way out is ultimately always fear: Fear of escalations, fear of not being taken seriously, fear of being hurt, fear of our own anger, and our partner's anger. It has its origins in childhood, either because we've copied certain behaviors from our parents or because we experienced something we haven't been able to shed to this day.

Children primarily learn through imitation and their own experiences. The behavior of one parent may also be replicated, even though time-delayed. For example, Marion's mother usually reacted with accusations when marital problems arose, and there were many fights. At first, her father was calm, but when it got too much for him, he fled. He slammed the door behind him and went to his friends at the club.

Marion greatly resembles her father. She, too, avoids confrontations. When problems arise with her partner, she leaves for the gym. In fact, no matter how hurt she is about something, she's unable to voice it—just as her father couldn't tell her mother how hurt he felt when she hurled accusations at him.

Our own experiences also shape our adult life. For example, as a child, Thomas often felt he wasn't being taken seriously. If something was difficult for him, his parents compared him to his younger brother, who was much better at it. As a consequence, he withdrew. Later, in a relationship with Ursula, he often didn't dare to say what was bothering him out of fear of being belittled again.

Getting wise to your escape hatches

Admitting to yourself or even noticing that you are looking for an escape hatch is a huge step, because it also means acknowledging your fear. It can be quite embarrassing, admitting fear. If it's not usual in your relationship to voice things openly, if you never learned it, then you have to approach this issue step by step.

In therapy, we ask couples when and how they use their escape hatches. In most cases, they know those of their partner better than their own. Sure, it's easier observing our partners than ourselves. However, it's vital to discover your own escape hatches.

The next step takes courage. To get in touch with your partner, you should talk about your fears. Tell him why you're taking a specific escape hatch. "I'd rather walk the dog than talk to you about my fears because I'm afraid you'll laugh at me." Or, "Whenever you want to talk to me about an argument, I'd rather go to the gym because I'm afraid your anger will hurt me even more."

As a partner, it's imperative to show special appreciation for such outing, because if your partner can bring him or herself to express their greatest vulnerability, they will need security. To say, "Well, what do you known, you finally caught on!" would be the worst thing you could do. Because then next time, they'll think twice before telling you something so intimate.

Behind the escape hatch is usually the hope for harmony. We are often unable to confront our partners openly because we never learned how, so this positive impulse is diverted towards an escape hatch. Unfortunately, as far as alcohol is concerned, in the beginning it might seem like a standard emergency measure. But later, it becomes routine and addictive, so that intimacy becomes impossible. The good news is, if both can find a way to identify the reasons, the result can be a bond that is deeper and more beautiful than ever before.

What It Was Really About

In the scene at the beginning of the chapter, it becomes clear that Sabine and Roland were using escape hatches. At first, they both used accusations as a way out. Sabine with the help of her friends: She complained to her friends in front of Roland: "I was afraid that Roland would dismiss my problem as nothing if I talked to him privately about it. That's why I wanted back-up."
Sabine had known that fear since childhood and had learned how to deal with it even then. When she needed her parents' help in school, she never dared to ask. Since she was the fourth child, it was expected that everything would go like clockwork. Had she asked her parents for help, she would have been afraid of hearing: "What? You can't do that yet? Let's hope you won't have to repeat the whole year!" They would have downplayed her problem. Even back then, she learned to share her problems with friends – just as she did in this scene.
Roland chose the accusation as an escape hatch as well. "Instead of telling Sabine how embarrassing it was for me to be exposed in front of friends, I accused her of being ungrateful. In my childhood, I was embarrassed in similar ways and had a hard time with it."
At the end of the scene, Roland uses a second escape hatch to avoid a discussion with Sabine; he worked longer hours than necessary to avoid getting home and having to talk with her.

Roland hadn't learned to spar directly with someone. When his parents fought, it was always behind closed doors.

Both of them were successful in preventing closeness. She couldn't tell him how alone and neglected she felt in her life. And he couldn't tell her how often he had been embarrassed and compromised. The energy they both felt—in the form of anger and humiliation—led them through back doors instead of concentrating on the relationship and having a clarifying conversation.

What You Can Do

🌱 Examine your escape hatches. What do you contribute to avoiding closeness? Try to cast aside all of your supposedly reasonable motivations for that back door (for example, that it could be a positive to spend more time with the children). Write up your behavior and find your "favorite escape hatch."

🌱 Try blocking your exit. Imagine that your favorite way out doesn't exist anymore and you can't use it whenever you want. For example, you can't do overtime at the office when there's a conflict waiting for you at home. You have to go home because the office building is closing down. What fears arise? Describe your anxiety on a piece of paper. Do these feelings remind you of something in your childhood?

🌱 During childhood, who did you see using the same escape hatch?

- How can you convey all this to your partner? What would it take to be able to talk about your favorite escape hatch? It might be that just thinking about it brings up your fears, and you're tempted again to look for a way out to avoid a confrontation. So, watch out that you don't outwit yourself.

- Find the right moment for a talk. It would be ideal if your partner would also talk about their escape hatches, but don't make that a condition. If you show your courage, your partner will find courage, too.

- Which alternatives are there to your old solutions? What small next step would you be willing to take, instead of using your original escape hatch? It might take some time for you to find such a step. Be patient with yourself. Instead of going to the gym, suggest jogging together (where you might find the time to talk).

8. Finally, Someone Understands Me

The three-way as an escape hatch out of relationship frustration

Roland and Sabine are on their way to a Mexican restaurant to meet friends for dinner.
"How was your therapy weekend?" Roland asks.
Sabine is silent.
"Hey, I asked you something."
"Come on; these things usually don't interest you."
"Of course I'm interested."
"So why didn't you ask me when I came back from the workshop? You're not really interested in what I'm learning. You're only ever interested in one thing."
"That's not true. But since you're bringing it up: did anything happen with a guy?"
Sabine takes a deep breath and falls silent. She's heard that question so often. Over and over again, she's had to listen to Roland's gloomy prediction that it's inevitable she'll cheat on him one day. That alone enrages her! Up to now, she was always able to reassure him. But this time...
"Yes. Something did," she finally blurts out.
Roland is stunned. He gets dizzy, as if the ground under his feet is shaking. A burning sensation creeps from his gut to his head.
"What...what did you say?" he stammers.
"You heard me."
"And you say it, just like that? Did you sleep with him?"

"Yes. And I don't care what happens next. I can't stand it anymore, the way you've been treating me lately."
They continue in silence. Roland is numb from shock. Sabine is consumed by anger and a guilty conscience.

The affair – A sign that something is missing in the relationship

Nobody ever wants to experience a situation like Sabine and Roland's. And if it does happen, for one of them the world collapses like a house of cards, the other one is torn between rage, despair and a guilty conscience. It seems absurd to try to wring anything positive from such a horror show, and yet, an affair is a cry for help. It's a sign that something urgently must be done for the relationship. Because in a successful, fulfilled relationship, there is no room for a third person. Perhaps one flirts with a colleague at work or the sister of a friend. But nothing will come of it, because a good relationship offers everything you need to be happy: security, passion, and trust sustain it. Heart and loin are connected.

When a relationship becomes shaky, a partner may flee and rush into an affair. Look at it from this perspective: it's as if both are on a speeding train. Each is too busy with everyday matters to realize the train is heading for an abyss until one of them notices and pulls the emergency brake. The affair, that's the emergency brake.

In reality, you'd never think of jumping out of a speeding train, each in a different direction of all things. On the contrary: facing the danger, you'd try everything to stop the train as quickly as possible. Only when the greatest danger had passed would you consider the next step to detour the train to reach your destination.

When it comes to a relationship, however, most people react differently. The first reflex, when confronted with an affair, is to skip out and leave, get a divorce or at least separate. If this occurs, all misunderstandings remain unsolved, all the pain and grief remains, and is usually carried on over to the next, new relationship.

Clarifying instead of escaping

Evasion is a natural reaction and, on the surface, understandable. If we've been hurt very badly, it's normal to try and avoid further pain. "You betrayed me with that man, so why don't you just stay with him. I want a divorce!" There is anger and defiance in that statement, and yet, it's quite understandable. It's a natural reaction to want to escape from such a relationship. But in most cases, the problems, conflicts, and unfulfilled desires repeat themselves in the next relationship. Then one is compelled to escape again and hope that the next relationship will bring better luck. But it's not so easy.

An affair shouldn't be the end, but the beginning of a process of development. Just as you'd pull the emergency brake on the train to stop it in case of danger, you can put a stop to an affair. Set aside all major decisions—separation, divorce. Defer them to a later date, after you've taken a close look at your relationship. An affair is a symptom, and it's worthwhile to search for the background and reasons leading up to it. You'll be surprised about the new things and insight you'll find out about your partner.

Admittedly, this is an extremely difficult task. Those who have sought fulfillment in an outside relationship usually believe themselves to have found what was missing in their partnership. To sit down and look for the good things in the old, tattered relationship and work towards a future together requires quite an effort. It's also difficult for the betrayed person. They will need a great deal of courage to find closeness with the person who initiated the hurt. And one also has to accept the affair as it is—for the time being. Every "I want you to stop seeing them" only leads to further resistance and pain.

"Yes, we have a serious problem and want to find out what happened," is the appropriate attitude. Take the time to clear things up. Find out why a third person had space in your relationship. The reward: You will reach a new, fulfilling level in your relationship. And if you do decide to separate, it will be with good feelings, and you can look toward a future without inherited burdens.

Crises require closeness – The clearing period

In the sixties and seventies, it was trendy for a couple in a crisis to separate "temporarily." One of the partners moved out. That's really problematic because nothing can be resolved in this way. If you had a conflict with one of your colleagues, you probably wouldn't try to solve the problem by avoiding that person. Complaining to friends about your miserable work situation wouldn't help either. It's better to clear things up with your colleague, then find a solution.

The same is true in a relationship. Each crisis requires the closeness of the people involved. It's the only way to communicate with each other. If, instead, you move out "temporarily," it'll only be more difficult to communicate.

Please take enough time to clear up the situation. An affair is often preceded by years of disappointments and misunderstandings. It takes just as much time to clear the couples interspace. Allow about four weeks of clearing time per year of the relationship. If that sounds unimaginably long to you, then please come to an agreement for a time period that is acceptable to both of you.

For Gabriel and Stephanie, it was hard to decide on a clearing period. They came to our practice when Stephanie found out about Gabriel's affair. At first, she demanded the obvious: "I'll only do couples therapy with you if you end the affair." Gabriel sat there, stone-faced and said it would be pointless, since he assumed that they would separate anyway. "She's just always sad and reproachful," he said. "I can't make her happy." Gabriel wasn't willing to end the affair. How could he be? He was petrified of never being able to have a happy relationship. In the new relationship, he seemed to have found it. Later on, it became evident that they had both contributed to this precarious situation. They were ready to take a closer look—with a happy ending.

Both are responsible for the misery

It's obvious that the person looking for an affair had their part in contributing to the crisis. What is less obvious is that the other person also contributed. Let's put it this way: if a person turns to someone outside the relationship, the other one has already withdrawn from it. When one turns to the outside, the other withdraws—therefore neither is approachable. Only when both sides accept the fact that they played a part can a solution be found.

Let's take another look at the lives of Stephanie and Gabriel. Two quite attractive people had found each other, and the erotic tension between them was palpable. However, they couldn't let it play out. She was too busy bombarding him with accusations, which petrified him.

During couples therapy, both were able to recognize their responsibility for the crisis. Stephanie realized that her continual admonitions made her less attractive to Gabriel, which was why he became detached. Stephanie was all too familiar with that reproachfulness from her mother, and had copied her behavior in subconscious loyalty. Gabriel realized that Stephanie had touched his sore spot, because his mother had often reprimanded him, too, which made him furious. We supported Gabriel in converting his anger: instead of unloading it in the affair, he could bring his wife back into the conversation. His petrification slowly weakened.

Embrace me, but don't get too close!

The interesting thing about a love triangle is that all three—no matter how different their aims may be—have something essential in common. All three are stuck in their dilemma: I'm longing for your closeness, but I'm afraid of it. This aspect should be acknowledged and looked at more closely.

Let's take a quick look at Stephanie and Gabriel's childhoods. Stephanie lost her father at an early age and suffered greatly because of it. Then, as a child, she subconsciously swore to herself: Never again will anyone come that close and then leave me. It's clear that Stephanie is afraid of closeness even though she's aching for it. So, what is her survival strategy? She escapes into blaming—copying her mother—thereby creating the necessary safety zone.

Gabriel was often disciplined as a child. To him, closeness meant discipline and blame. His survival strategy as a child was: Escape to the soccer field. Now he's hearing the recriminations from his wife instead of his parents. And where does he escape to now? Into an affair

Finally, the third person has a wish for closeness, and at the same time a fear of it. By choosing a man who's not available, she makes sure in her own way to rule out too much closeness. On the one hand, she wishes for nothing more than a permanent relationship, but on the other hand, she's afraid of it. It's astonishing how often such people repeatedly choose a partner who's already in a relationship. One might say, they're sitting between two chairs and operating between two people—perhaps because they once had that role with their parents.

What does she have that I don't?

Should you be confronted with such a terrible crisis, you might ask yourself: what does that person have that I don't? Is she younger, prettier, slimmer, does she have a better job than me? Is she better in bed? One could brood for nights on end over such questions. Competition and jealousy eat at the soul, rob you of sleep, and gnaw on your self-esteem.

That won't get you anywhere. These thoughts only make you angry, depressed, jealous; they make you feel inferior. The right question is: What does that person provide that we don't express in our relationship? As soon as you ask yourself that question, you open a window to a new dimension.

When Stephanie considered the question, it became clear: years ago, she had already given up on the joy in her relationship. By working at trying to bring this joy back into her life, the connection, so to speak, became whole once more, and there was no room left for an outside relationship.

Children fight: for Mom, for Dad, and to keep the family together

For children, it's especially challenging when one of their parents has an affair. Children have a subconscious inclination to protect their parents' relationship. They fight on three fronts simultaneously: for their parents as a couple, and for Mom and Dad individually. For the child, this has several consequences: typically, they lean more to one side than the other, depending on whom they consider weaker. Should the marriage fail, the children often take responsibility for it and subconsciously feel guilty about the separation. Usually, they carry that guilt up to their adulthood – which often dooms their own relationships.

That's why it's so important to clarify your relationship. You help not only yourself but also your children. Set a positive example when it comes to crisis management and relationship building, and clear up what stands between you. Even if your marriage ultimately ends in divorce, children can acquire the ability to handle difficult life situations constructively.

During a marriage crisis, it's especially important to make it clear to the children that they don't need to drag around a guilty conscience, and that the crisis must be handled exclusively by the two adults. It's not enough to tell them: "it's got nothing to do with you." More than the words, it's the atmosphere that children retain in their system.

We have had good experiences with couples that informed their children about their love triangle. They can't conceal the crisis; the children sense it anyway. Many children are relieved by an open discussion, as your clear message can dispel their fears. It's not necessary to go into details, but pay attention to your wording. Confront the children as parents: "We are in a difficult crisis. There is another woman involved, but we're working on clearing that up. We promise that we'll handle this together until we find a good solution." Also, communicate your sympathy for your children's situation. "We understand that you're afraid we might separate. But we promise you we'll take the time to find a good solution."

Crises as the engine of development processes

Everyone can experience a crisis, at any age. And each time, you come up against physical or emotional barriers that can help you to grow. You are confronted with uncharted territory and you're forced to put long-standing behaviors to the test—and if necessary, to adapt them. In this way, you expand the space you have to maneuver and you are better equipped to cope with the next crisis.

An affair is an especially dramatic crisis for a couple. Many fears, hardships, expectations, longings, shame, and hurt pride accompany those who come to our practice. The most crucial decision at that point is: Do we want to overcome the crisis and ensure the next step in our personal development? If you fail to take that chance, you're relinquishing a learning process that would provide you with a valuable impetus in your life. We genuinely hope you find the courage to take an honest look and create a solid foundation for continued self-development.

What It Was Really About

Sabine had an affair, but the crisis originated much earlier in the relationship. At that time, Roland was heavily involved in the family business. "Daily brooding about how to keep the company afloat took almost all the energy out of the relationship. Also, I had no idea how strenuous and challenging psychotherapy training could be. The topic didn't interest me that much. At times, the training sessions brought Sabine to the edges of what her personality could handle. I should have supported her more, but I was so absorbed in my work that I could not really feel myself or my wife."

Roland had learned that buckling down, ambition, diligence, and teamwork are exceptional values. These qualities made him successful as far as his profession was concerned. But his needs and those of his relationship remained undiscovered. "I never learned to stop and look into what was happening in the relationship."

Sabine, in turn, had her father as a role model. He withdrew when there were marital conflicts. Instead of confronting his wife, he fled to his firm, and sometimes to affairs with other women.

"I never confronted Roland about the fact that he was withdrawing from our relationship," Sabine said. "I felt very alone. But I accepted it and never even thought of confronting Roland with it. Instead, I looked for someone else and started an affair with him."

Fortunately, Roland and Sabine were ready for couples therapy, which they engaged in regularly for two years and in which they were able to lay the foundation for their future relationship.

What You Can Do

🌱 If you're stuck in a love triangle, you're in a crisis that is hard to manage alone. The support of an Imago therapist might possibly be the most efficient route to take.

🌱 Agree on a period in which you can review the status quo and take a good look at your crisis. A written agreement would be best.

For the one having an affair
- When did the crisis begin?
- What was missing to make you look for fulfillment with this third person?
- What were the things you avoided talking about in the past few months with your partner? Which desires did you not mention, even though you were frustrated?
- What has your partner contributed to your going astray?
- Think back, maybe even to the beginning of your relationship. At what point did you experience with your partner what you are now experiencing in your affair?
- Look for a quiet spot and take half an hour in which you close your eyes and imagine two alternatives:
    1. You choose your new partner. Be honest and consider the following: how would your life continue in

detail? What would your life be like in five, ten, fifteen years? How much contact would you have with your former partner?

2. You decide to remain with your current partner. You master the crisis. How would your relationship look like in detail? Use the same parameters as above.

Trust your subconscious. It may provide you with the next impulses and directions.

For the betrayed one

🌱 When did the crisis most likely start? It might be quite some time back. What exactly happened then?

🌱 Be honest with yourself and figure out when you withdrew from the relationship and focused your energy somewhere else. Where did it go?

🌱 What part did you play in pushing your partner into distancing him/herself? Be honest with yourself, without self-reproach or guilt.

🌱 What do you need to find yourself again? What can you do to achieve this?

🌱 What's missing in your relationship? What can you do to retrieve whatever is missing? If you've had a tough time getting close to your partner in the past months, take heart and seek out that closeness again.

For the third person

- Is it a coincidence, or is there any deeper meaning in the fact that you fell in love with someone who is in a relationship? Are there love triangles in your family – with your parents' or other family members?

- Have you ever fallen in love before with a person who was already in a relationship? Think about whether there is a clear tendency (consciously or subconsciously) to remain in a love triangle.

- How much time and space are you willing to give your new partner, first to sort out the old relationship, and then to consider whether or not to enter a new relationship with you? Are you willing to set an appropriate time period together?

After the crisis: you decide to part ways

- Organize an emotional farewell with professional help (see Chapter 12).

- One of the best forces for further development is mutual forgiveness. It has been our experience that in the majority of cases, this is only possible with professional help. Don't just forgive the other one, but also yourself for whatever you contributed to the separation.

- If you are parents, try to maintain the respect you always had for the other person. You are responsible for your children, so be a good role model for the next generation.

After the crisis: you decide to stay together

🌱 Find a good way to bid the third person with whom you possibly spent an intensive time farewell. For example, write a farewell letter, whether you mail it or not, or decide on a farewell ritual (see Chapter 12) that is acceptable to both of you.
If you are the person who has been betrayed, try to be respectful to the third person and consider them as an important part of your shared relationship history.

🌱 If you are the third person, try to find a good way to say goodbye instead of withdrawing in anger and rage. Try to respect and value the time you spent together.

🌱 Forgiveness is an important basis for your future. This is true for both because you both played a part in letting the outside relationship happen. Allow some time to pass to resolve the past and to forgive yourself. Only then will you really be free to trust each other again.

9. I Want to Become a Better Person for You

Love means trying out something new for your partner's sake

Sabine and Roland are getting ready for a party, when Sabine comes out of the bedroom in a turquoise blouse and skirt with flower pattern, Roland whistles.
"Where did you get that pretty blouse? You look great!"
"You think so? I'm not sure; it's very...floral."
"Well, I like it!"
Sabine plucks uncertainly at her blouse. She feels better in unobtrusive colors, but appreciates Roland's compliments. Indecisive, she returns to the bedroom.
Twenty minutes later it's time to leave, and Roland finds Sabine in the bathroom – in a gray skirt and gray sweater, with only a hint of turquoise peeking out at the collar.
"Sabine, what's that? Why gray in gray? The colors before were much nicer!"
"Oh, leave me alone. It's the first time those people have invited us, and I don't want to be so dressed up."
"But now you look mousy! I don't like that at all."
"And I don't like you always nagging me!"
"But I just told you before how pretty you looked in those lovely colors. And now? Totally nondescript. I'm really frustrated!"
Sabine is offended. "I'm frustrated, too. Either we go to the party as I am, or you go alone."

Embrace Conflict

Harmonious relationships are nice. You don't fight, and if you disagree, you give in and swallow your own wishes rather than confronting your partner with them. And you are proud to have a "functioning" marriage, because quarrels are considered a failure. That's how it can happen that in time you stop communicating. Because avoidance means gridlock, and in the end, often separation.

If you want a healthy and lively relationship, then be open about disagreements. Welcome them, because conflicts give you a chance to develop. Whenever frustration arises, energy also arises, and this energy makes movement possible. So, use the conflict to keep your relationship alive and developing.

90:10 – The Twin Pack

If a particular behavior of your partner frustrates you again and again, you can be sure that a part of your life history is behind it. At some point in your childhood, you must have been frustrated similarly, making you especially sensitive. Had you not had that childhood experience, you'd have no problem with your partner's "strange" behavior. Instead of being frustrated, you'd either meet such behavior with sympathy—or pay no attention to it at all.

Any frustration tells us more about ourselves than about the quality of the relationship. 90 percent can be attributed to our past, and only 10 percent to the present situation in which the frustration has come to light. This means that if you look for the reason behind the conflict, for one thing you will have healed a part of your life history, and for another, you'll have immediately resolved the conflict in your relationship. Isn't that great?

This 90:10 rule has another significant advantage. If you're the one who is frustrated with your partner, then you now know that 10 percent of the frustration concerns you both. The rest has to do with their past. That's a relief to know. However, you were the catalyst. And you can be sure that you, too, will find an experience in your childhood that is the origin of the current conflict.

A Double Gift

You are both giving each other a gift if you clear up your frustration together. You get the chance to trace the cause back to its origin and thereby heal old wounds. At the same time, you'll be able to solve that conflict in your relationship permanently.

The gift for the frustrated one

The actual poison that sickens a relationship is not so much the frustration itself, but rather what the frustrated person interprets in the behavior of the partner. An example: Whenever Hans and Gerda meet, she arrives late. Hans is frustrated because he thinks, "she's late because I'm not important to her." So, it's not the lateness, but the feeling of being unimportant that bothers Hans. Another example: Susanne would love to play squash every weekend, but Peter is against it. Susanne's interpretation is: I'm not considered worthy of having my own space. That hurts more than the fact that she's not able to pursue her hobby.

Your interpretation is the doorway to your childhood history. It might involve conscious experiences or subconscious feelings. Usually, the frustrating situations and the corresponding childhood experiences aren't identical. Only the feelings that arose in childhood are the same as in the current conflict. Hans interpreted Gerda's lateness as disrespect and that made him feel inferior. The reason for this interpretation isn't necessarily that his father was always late but rather that his parents generally didn't take their children's needs into account for example.

Leaving behind recriminations

"You cannot heal what you do not feel," this English epigram best expresses why we need our love partners in order to heal. Hans already felt inferior when he was single. But no one had frustrated him the way Gerda did, so he didn't feel the need to investigate it. Only since Gerda entered his life, and pushed the same buttons over and over again, could he feel the pain he experienced as a child.

It was now up to the frustrated one to recognize his 90 percent portion of the quarrel and slowly let go of the blame game with his partner. That's the great challenge, because it certainly is easier to make accusations than to face the childhood pain at the other end of the 90 percent share.

Gerda helped Hans with that task. During couples therapy, Hans remembers: "I feel small and inferior when Gerda is late. That's how I felt when I built great things with my toys, and my mother never had time to praise me. She always put me off until later—but she hardly ever came!" Hans's story helped Gerda to understand his problem, and Hans was able to dissolve his old pain. That's the gift Hans received.

The gift for the one who frustrates

Your partner catches you right where, in the course of your development, you had to "twist" yourself to ensure your survival. Gerda, for example, might have developed a strong desire for freedom during her childhood—possibly because she felt penned up too often, or constantly monitored. Her survival pattern: you're entitled to the time you take; don't let anyone rush you. That's why she is late so often.

Only, that pattern does not liberate her now. Not only because Hans gripes, but also because being late for professional appointments has even been detrimental to her at times. Those are good occasions to question whether Gerda still needs that pattern of survival today.

Patterns of survival are great

Imagine you injure your foot and you're struggling to get from one place to the next on crutches. In time you'll learn to handle them; your arm and shoulder muscles develop, and you can keep your balance when climbing stairs. Walking with crutches becomes so normal that, even after your foot heals, you're still using them and don't even notice. Only the people around you wonder why you're acting so strangely.

The same is true for patterns of survival. They emerged in childhood situations when you were overwhelmed and had to look for "crutches" to cope. These are vital for children. When Gerda activates her crutches, that is, she is late, she is using an old survival pattern from her youth. Gerda's greatest challenge is also her gift. If she drops her crutches, she increases her elbow room. She can be on time when it's important, or she can be more lax about it. In that way, she has given herself a lot more freedom.

Unlearning and Learning—And Making Room for Something New

If, from one day to the next, you take the crutches away from someone who has been using them for much too long, he'll fall over. It's the same with patterns of survival. Throwing them overboard immediately creates fear and leads to denial. We would much rather stick to our old habits! They are stored in our limbic system, in the section where our experiences and fears are recorded. Our brains can immediately assess whether a situation is dangerous or not, and they contain reflexes ready to react quickly.

These reflexes surface arbitrarily, and we can hardly prevent them in these situations. If you want to unlearn such reflexes in the long term, you need to be very secure. You can give that to each other by cooperating insightfully and effectively. Make sure the first steps are small so they will lead to success. Even the smallest sense of achievement encourages the next small step.

Small steps at the growth border

The growth border is the point where one's greatest desire encounters the other's greatest need. Hans's biggest wish: "I want Gerda to be on time to prove that I'm important to her." That wish collides with Gerda's greatest need: the space to move and breathe.

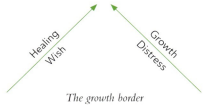

The growth border

If the one who caused the frustration can change his behavior step by step, the frustrated one can heal. At the same time, the frustrated one learns to overcome distress and transform the survival mode into a healthy mode. The current trouble spot in the partnership, as well as the childhood pain, are healed.

Expressing a request: positive, concrete, and measurable

Hans would like Gerda never to be late again. As the frustrated one, he has a strong yearning to heal; that's why he's constantly upset. Gerda, on the other hand, has to defend her survival pattern, so they argue regularly. The way out of that unpleasant situation is for Hans to formulate his plea.

"Sure," Hans says immediately. "Please don't ever be so late again." That's a very big request and formulated much too vaguely, meaning Gerda would definitely be swamped.

Formulate positively: If Hans says, Gerda should never be so late again, he is formulating negatively. "Too late" is in that request—and that's what sticks. Because our brains have a hard time digesting negative formulations, it would have to think outside the box. So, it would be better for Hans to ask Gerda to "be punctual from now on."

Formulate concretely: different people might understand the same subject differently. Even "punctual" can be interpreted in different ways. Some people think they are punctual if they're ten minutes early. Others think it's more polite to be half an hour late. Therefore, it's not enough to say "please be punctual," but "please come at 6 p.m."

Formulating measurably: Pleas need a beginning and an end. Only then can both recognize whether they were successful. It's Hans's great wish that Gerda will always arrive at the agreed-upon time. But at which point in time would they both be content with their success, and even celebrate a little? Gerda certainly needs to be motivated to make the next step easier. She wants to be able to say: "Great! I did it"!

"Please, for the next three weeks, be at the bar of the dance class five minutes before it begins, with your dancing shoes on!" That request has everything necessary to be able to realize it so that you can celebrate your first feelings of success.

Being able to accept and endure gifts

The behavior change is a gift from the person who caused the frustration. The most challenging task for the frustrated one is to accept and endure it. Some sabotage themselves at this point, for example, by downplaying the successful first step and sweeping it aside as hardly worth mentioning.

Why do we react like that? If Hans is at the agreed meeting point on time and Gerda arrives punctually, he'll suddenly feel what he missed so much as a child: esteem. At the same time, the pain sets in—and sometimes, it's so hard to take that it has to be deflected. It's a paradox that we feel pain and sadness at a point where we received such a special gift. And still, that's the way it is.

It's worth accepting the gift and enduring whatever feelings arise. That's the only way the brain learns to redirect neural connections, and a part of the wound is healed.

Stretch your emotional muscle

It's challenging even for the person wishing to fulfill the request. It's necessary to try something new, with which you have had no experience. At the same time, you must give up something old that has become so familiar.

Imago calls it *stretching* when something new is being attempted and you have to endure the emerging emotions. If Gerda accommodates Hans by fulfilling his plea, she stretches her "emotional muscle," so to speak. What does that mean? You might feel a sense of security by using the familiar crutches, but through the years of use, some of your emotional muscles have shortened. If we let go of the crutches for a bit, we stretch that shortened muscle a little as well, and the next step is somewhat easier. You discover that there are positive sides to walking without crutches, too.

What It Was Really About

Roland and Sabine experienced the scene described at the beginning of the chapter many times. Roland would have loved to see his wife in lively colors, and regularly caused Sabine distress because she was afraid of being too conspicuous. With the help of an Imago therapist, they discovered the origin.
Do you recognize the couple's growth border? Roland's greatest wish—to make Sabine happy—provokes her greatest distress: The fear of attracting attention and possibly offending. "When I came upon Sabine in the bathroom and saw that she had dressed gray on gray again, I was frustrated," Roland recounts. Not so much because of the change in wardrobe, but because of the way he interpreted her actions. "My interpretation was: I can't make her happy. Subconsciously it reminded me of the pain in my childhood. My father was extremely depressed, which often clouded the atmosphere. Like many other children, I took on the responsibility of my father's unhappiness. The fact that I

wasn't able to make him feel good created immense frustrations within me."

Sabine also reacted frustrated to Roland's disappointment. She felt she was being pushed into something that didn't suit her. Even though she initially put on the flowered skirt and colored blouse, her old behavior pattern struck, and she changed into inconspicuous colors.

For Sabine as a child, it was difficult to be visible. "My parents fought a lot, and it was dangerous for my brothers and me to get between those permanent power struggles. Being inconspicuous was the safest way for me to survive. My older brother Tom handled it differently. He fought with my mother for recognition—and often got a beating for it. One more reason for me to remain invisible!" she said.

As an adult, when she had to meet new people, she was always afraid of being visible, saying something wrong, or attracting any negative attention. She felt safe in unobtrusive clothes. So, when she had to accompany Roland to the party, it wasn't her intention to hurt his feelings but to protect herself.

What You Can Do

Training sequence for the frustrated one
1. Interpretation: Which frustrating situation keeps repeating in your relationship?
2. How do you interpret it? What does it say about you?
3. Childhood: Which feeling arises with that frustration? Does it seem familiar from your childhood? The first image that emerges will be the right one!
4. Requests: Close your eyes for a moment and feel what your greatest wish is from your partner. Formulate three requests that are positive, concrete, and measurable.
5. Accept: Imagine what might happen if your partner fulfills your wishes. How will it feel? What will feel good? What might not?
6. Boycott: The final question might be a paradox. More often than not, we boycott the fulfillment of our requests. That's what you would do if at last your partner arrived punctually, and you said: "Let's see if that wasn't just a one-off." You'd be downplaying the effort, and you'd both be disappointed. So, prepare yourself to handle it if your wish is fulfilled!

Training sequence for the one causing the frustration
1. Background: Reflect on why you don't change the behavior that keeps frustrating your partner. To what extent are you acting somewhat childish compared to a mature adult?
2. Patterns of survival: What deep anguish hides behind

the fact that you keep having to behave in this way? Which fear hides behind it? Which fear arises when you imagine changing that part?

3. Role model: Do you recognize your behavior from within your family? Is there someone who exhibited precisely this behavior or the exact opposite? What does that person mean to you? Would you like to be closer to that person?
4. Cost: Gather ideas. What's missing in your life if you stick to this behavior? What's missing in your relationship because of it?
5. Freedom: Which energies and potentials are liberated within you if you make concessions to your partner? Which fears do you have to overcome that you may have learned in your childhood, if you comply with your partner's request?
6. Trust: What kind of trust do you regain by complying in that way?

10. Just Last Summer I Told My Wife that I Love Her

Love is an activity, not a state

"Who could that be?" Sabine wonders when the doorbell rings in the late afternoon of her birthday. When she notices Roland's playful innocent look, she raises her eyebrow in alarm.

She opens the door—and Rudi, Roland's best friend, hands her a birthday cake. "Happy 22nd!"

"What...why?" Sabine stammers. "How did you know it's my birthday?" Shyly she takes the cake and gives him an embarrassed smile.

Then, the bell rings again. Sabine looks at Roland in shock; he can hardly keep from grinning broadly. Christa, Sasha, Larry, Sanna, and other friends are at the door.

"What are you doing here?"

"Celebrating your birthday, of course! All the best, dear Sabine!" Sabine, numb and speechless, accepts kisses and flowers.

"What's this all about?" She sternly whispers into Roland's ear as they walk towards the living room. Roland, who spent weeks imagining how happy Sabine would be with this surprise, is irritated about her angry look. "Well, it's my birthday present. A surprise party!"

At 2:30 in the morning, after the guests have left, Sabine blurts out: "What was the big idea inviting so many people? You know I can't stand crowds!"

"But I wanted to give you a very special present. It's mean that you don't appreciate it. I've worked on it for months. Everyone kept it a secret to make you happy, and now this! I'd be thrilled if you'd ever do something like that for me. But you'd never think of it."

Love wants to be shaped and developed

As long as we feel the butterflies in the first months of a relationship, all our sensors are extended, making it possible for us to read each wish off the lips of our loved one. We strive to be generous, loving, helpful and seductive, and it usually works. We're especially attentive, and our thoughts continuously whirl around that beloved person. We want to make them happy and be happy as well— forever. That's how we imagine true love to be, when one knows what the other one wants and needs, when you understand each other without having to verbalize it, that's pure seventh heaven!

Yes, we can hear you sighing now. If only that would last! You've probably had the experience that it doesn't work that way. When the daily routine slowly but surely creeps in, and the antennas shift to their standard frequency, we are often disappointed by love, by fate, by our partners. That's because of a misconception. We believe that lasting love is a matter of luck. Either we found the right partner, or not, and if not, it was bad luck, and we have to go on looking.

In fact, love is not a state, but an activity. Love, true love wants to be shaped and developed. And: There is no such thing as "the" love. Each couple has their own version and has to shape it in their own way. It's a lot like flowers, for which there is also not one single formula for them to flourish. Each flower has its particular needs. An orchid, for example, needs damp, loose soil and a spot protected from the sun. A ponytail palm prefers dryness and direct sunlight. So, if you love your flowers, you have to nurse them individually, according to their needs.

It's not enough to take love for granted. You have to do something, and in order to do the right thing, you have to find out what both of you need to feel loved. And don't think that you both need exactly the same thing!

Different strokes for different folks

You might be familiar with the story about the wife who, for breakfast, gives her husband the top part of the roll each day, because she thinks he likes that. After thirty years, when they finally talk about it, they find out that the man eats the top only because he thinks she prefers the bottom, which isn't true at all. Since then, they each prepare their own breakfast roll.

That's typical: We show love the way we wish to receive it, thinking our partners have the same preferences. Out of love, you phone your partner at the office every day and then you're surprised to learn that it's seen as a disturbance rather than a sign of love. Or you bring home flowers every week, and then find out that they're thrown out before they've even wilted.

Tell me that you love me

You could call it a prank of nature that we often want something that means hell to our partners. In our practice, we regularly see this with couples. Physical contact is a good example: One of them needs it like the air they breathe, the other one has trouble coping with it, and prefers to express love verbally.

Speaking of verbalizing: Those three magic words, "I love you," are easy for some to say, while others can hardly get them out. Both are often misinterpreted. When we tell someone "I love you," it's just as much or as little proof of love as not being able to say it is proof of a lack of love.

And yet, that small sentence is something very special. It's charged with emotion and creates unique vibrations. Some couples might formulate it differently, but its magic is quite exceptional. Even a term of endearment—at the right time and place and in the right tone—might have that effect. On the other hand, it's very clear: Understanding love as an activity takes more than just loving words.

Asking and questioning

When we suggest, in our practice, that partners ask one another what they want from each other, we always hear the objection: "It can't be true love if I have to tell them what I want." The idea that love is perfect when we can read each other's lips is persistent.

The point is: When we don't ask for and talk about things, there's always the danger of being misunderstood. Or even doing something that has the opposite effect than we intend. It might be that you'll correctly interpret "that look she always puts on when I want to have sex." But it's a lot more likely that there are completely different and deeper reasons why she prefers physical distance.

Our preferences for how we want to be shown love have their origins early in our lives. An example: For Barbara, the best thing is to spend an evening with her lover, Klara—an evening where Klara has time just for her and no one else. An evening at a quiet place, where they talk, perhaps have a bite to eat, a glass of wine, where she is the most important thing and the center of attention. That wish is very understandable if you know that Barbara was raised in a large family with five siblings, where something was always going on and she rarely got individual attention. Klara, on the other hand, feels especially loved when she's in bed with Barbara and they are physically as close as possible. That, too, is understandable: Klara was an only child who received a great deal of attention, but whose parents were physically distant and did very little cuddling.

Ask your partner how she experienced love as a child. What was good, what was missing? You'll be surprised how easy it is to find out what your partner wants and especially needs.

Give me five!

Negative behavior, complaining, indifference, and angry outbursts infringe on the couples' interspace. One rule in this regard is of particular importance: The 5:1 rule. For each adverse action, there should be at least five positive behaviors on the same day. That way, you can create a harmonious balance that is good for the relationship.

So, the next time your partner complains, raise your hand for a high five. You'll see how that can change your life.

The Five Love Languages

Love is an activity we can shape, and not a state that befalls us. There are five basic forms you can focus on, and that can serve as an impetus for you.

Gifts and surprises

When it comes to presents, we usually think of various occasions like Christmas, birthdays, anniversaries. We think about meaningful gifts and awkward gifts. And we think of presents that make us happy because they are worthwhile.

We have some suggestions for gifts that are meaningful, surprising, and actually bring joy. A principle applies here, too: Don't conflate yourself with your partner. If you like sweets but your partner prefers salty, spicy food, don't give chocolates. Think about what your partner likes—or ask for a list you might use on different occasions.

Be selfless with your presents. If you give your lover chocolates hoping to eat them yourself, you've only done yourself a favor. And if your partner's not crazy about sports, but you like working out at the fitness club, a pair of athletic pants won't be the right gift.

Make your presents anti-cyclical. If you want to enrich your relationship, don't give only at traditional occasions, but also in between. You'll always have the benefit of surprise on your side.

Gifts don't have to be expensive—in fact, they don't need to cost anything. Surprise your partner with a spontaneous walk after a day at the office, just the two of you. Or give her a new writing pad because you know she always needs one.

Physical contact

For one person, a pat on the shoulder feels just right, and someone else might like to feel a hand on their back. In any case, it would be good to get a response. Try to notice how your partner reacts to a hug.

Many people had little physical contact during childhood

and need it urgently. Someone who opens his arms and says, "Come into my arms!" gives the other one the feeling that body contact is welcome. At the same time, some people experienced physical violence, assault, or abuse during childhood. They are often ambivalent about physical contact. If this is the case, it's important to be sensitive to your partner's reaction when there is a hug or other type of physical contact.

Adults often aren't sensitive enough to their children's needs. This makes an exchange all the more important to find out which type of physical affection to give to each other, and where there is potential for development. For example, to John, physical contact with Susan is important, especially when other people are around. When they meet friends, he likes to hold her hand, put his arm around her shoulder, or hug her now and then. Susan lets him do as he likes, but would prefer such gestures in a more intimate atmosphere.

It would be good for both if they oriented themselves on each other and developed a bit further. For example, the next time the couple meets friends at a restaurant, John puts his arm around Susan's shoulder. She could put her hand on his knee – even if just for a moment. On the other hand, it would be good for John not to overdo it so that Susan can feel comfortable.

A special form of physical contact is sex. The reason it's so special is that we are naked. We drop our last protective covers. That makes us especially vulnerable. Basically, sex is a straightforward matter, yet intimacy and sexuality in a relationship are very complex and multilayered. Chapter 11 will deal exclusively with this topic.

Appreciation and compliments

"But sweetheart, I just told you last year that I love you. Of course, I love you!" Even if you feel it's clear that you love your partner, say it more often. Repeat it even when it appears to be self-evident.

In case these three words are hard for you to say, there are many other ways to express your appreciation: "You look great in that shirt." Or: "Excellent, how you just convinced our little guy to eat those boiled carrots." Or: "Thank you for being in such a good mood today. It blew away my dark thoughts!"

One important suggestion: Always formulate your compliments and appreciation positively, otherwise a hidden reproach might resonate between the lines, and this expression of love would be for naught. "Positively" means avoiding words like "no" and "not." An example: "I appreciated that you didn't nag all day, and you didn't scowl." That's not appreciation, but rather pointing out how the other one usually acts. Try it positively: "Great that you're so lively today—your eyes are sparkling!"

It's also good to state your appreciation precisely and concretely. "It was nice watching you playing and laughing with the kids in bed this morning." In that way, your partner can visualize the scene, and it's easier for him/her to remember what it was you liked.

Even the tone is important when making compliments. Try out this phrase: "Hi Maria, great that you're here!" in various tones: Warm and loving, impatient and rapid, business-like, with a smile on your face, with a strained expression. Can you feel the difference? A loving tone adds a lot to help the other person feel more bonded with you.

You can also show your appreciation in writing. A message

like "Just thinking of you and looking forward to our evening," can be read and enjoyed by your loved one even during a meeting. Or you write "Hi, sweetie-pie" on a piece of paper and stick it on the make-up mirror. Or you scribble "I love you" on the edge of the shopping list, because you know today it's his shopping day.

Speaking of "sweetie pie." Terms of endearment or pet names are a loving way of showing closeness—if they're appreciated. For some, they've been carrying such nicknames since childhood and not a good fit anymore. Little Susie has grown up in the meantime and feels much more respected as Susan. We've also heard about terms of endearment that are hard to identify as such. Andrew, for example, called his loved one "Toad" in the beginning. He put all his emotional intensity into that name when saying it, but Isabella was horrified. Different strokes for different folks! Hence, our appeal: Ask if the term of endearment is welcome.

Time for each other—exclusively

In a world dominated by media, there is often little time for the relationship. The ring of a cell phone interrupts conversations. You want to watch the news and see the film after it, but though you are together, the focus is on the TV. The kids want their parents' attention. Overtime is the order of the day at work, or there's an urgent task to finish over the weekend.

So, it becomes more important than ever to find "time islands" for yourselves, even if only for half an hour. Emilia and Daniel, for example, meet each evening after the kids are in bed at their "smoking window" to have a cigarette and talk. They've been doing this for years, and even though they quit smoking a long time ago, they hold on to this ritual with that one cigarette. The entire family knows about the "smoking window," and even the kids understand that this is an inviolable space where they can't be disturbed.

Of course, time is spent together watching a movie on TV or going to the park with the kids. But the focus is on something different. An exclusive time slot means that there are only the two of you, and your attention is 100 percent on each other.

Helpfulness

The question "Can I help you?" shows your affection. The question "How can I help you?" makes it even clearer that you're standing at the starting gate, ready to support your loved one. Of course, both questions are proof of your love only if they're meant seriously and asked without any subliminal meaning.

If your partner is ill, you should certainly also ask what you can do. But especially when we're sick, it's sometimes challenging to formulate our wishes. You should take that into account in the event of illness. "I'll bring you the thermometer, and if you like, tea as well," is a concrete offer to which the poor coughing, sniffling creature in front of you only has to answer yes or no.

Of course, it's helpful when four hands are at the ready, instead of just two. But what's even more important is the feeling you convey with your willingness to help: You're not alone! That's why it's sort of sad when your partner doesn't want to help out in the kitchen, or car care is always left to the same person.

Help can also consist of listening. That, perhaps, is the most important form of being helpful. If your partner has a problem — with parents, on the job, etc., then your open ear is the best token of love. It makes your partner feel that you're there for her, and she will have a better chance of solving the problem easily and with confidence.

What It Was Really About

What happens if someone gives a present they would have liked to have received? It ensures disappointment. Roland thought of a surprise as the best present. That's why he organized that party for Sabine's birthday, without considering that Sabine hated such parties like the plague.
Roland's childhood was characterized by clear structures and defined rules which provided a lot of security. Something as unsure as a surprise happened only rarely. Therefore, little Roland was thrilled when his uncle came to visit from the States. "He lifted me onto his shoulders and just walked off. For me, that was a real adventure; at the same time, I loved getting all that attention." From such happy moments, a deep desire emerged in Roland to be surprised over and over again.
"When I organized Sabine's birthday party, I should have considered that it was my desire that I was transferring to Sabine. It would have been smarter to think about whether it was the right present for Sabine," Roland says today.
There was a great deal of tension and conflict between Sabine's parents. To get a lot of attention could be nice for a moment. But it was safer not to attract attention. "I have two older brothers who felt the full weight of my mother's strictness. When I was born, she was a little more relaxed. That was often enough

to make my brothers jealous. When I got attention, I often felt guilty about my brothers."

When Roland gave her the surprise party, all her fears arose again that someone might envy her for all that attention. "It was up to me to learn to accept what is given with love. And that I don't take anything away from anyone else if I'm given love."

Twenty years later, Roland again dared to surprise Sabine with a similar party—and this time, Sabine was pleased about it and able to accept Roland's appreciation entirely.

What You Can Do

🌱 Make a note of ten ways that you would like to be surprised. That might be something material—flowers, a book, etc. —or something immaterial—being picked up from the office, a call, etc. Ask your partner to do the same.

🌱 For two weeks, write daily notes about what you appreciate or love about your partner, independent of whether that behavior or characteristic is apparent at the moment or not. Write a daily note containing an expression of appreciation and stick it on a spot where they are sure to see it. Differentiate between character and behavior: "I like your sense of humor" is appreciation for a characteristic. "I appreciate that you accompanied me to my family last weekend" is appreciation for behavior.

Leave these notes of appreciation even if your partner irritated you on a given day. That helps to keep the focus on the positive.

🌱 Ask your partner to tell you about their childhood celebrations. Which were particularly enjoyable and which were not? What is especially important to them today?

🌱 Together, consider which rituals are coming up in your relationship: an anniversary, the imminent birth of a child, a wedding?

🌱 Talk about activities you used to like but have stopped doing. When was the last time you went to a dance class, a concert, a movie?

11. Sex, Or the Simplest Thing in the World

Passion requires security

As they do every year, Sabine and Roland go skiing during winter vacation along with their children and friends. The first evening they are all sitting together, making plans for the next day; they have a lively conversation and there's plenty of laughter. Again and again, Roland has to stroke Sabine's hair, kiss and touch her. He's so thrilled that they're all together and he can be close to his loved ones.
"I love you," he tells Sabine on the way to the room. "I'm happy that we're having such a good time."
"Mhmm...oh, I'm so tired! I'm looking forward to bed. It was a strenuous day."
"Sweetheart, I'm also looking forward to bed, and especially what we can do there!"
Upstairs in the room, Sabine says: "I really feel sick. I think I ate too much. And I'm exhausted!"
While Sabine goes to the bathroom, Roland lies down on the bed in frustration and turns on the TV.
"That's nice. You want to watch TV?" Sabine says.
"I don't want to watch TV. I want to have sex with you. But obviously, it doesn't fit into your agenda again."
"But that's not fair! Besides, I've been annoyed with you for a while, so why would I want to have sex with you?"
"What do you mean by annoyed? About what?"
"All I can say is: the stereo system."

"Oh, come on! I thought that was all cleared up!"
"What do you mean, 'cleared up'? You bought a stereo system without consulting me. You just ignored me and decided everything yourself. As if I didn't count!"
"Interesting how these things always occur to you when we could be having sex."
"I don't want to sleep with you if you ignore me like that!"
"And I thought you don't want sex because you ate too much!"

The simplest thing in the world?

Opinions are divided as to whether sex is the simplest thing in the world or the most complicated. Ultimately, there are many different viewpoints: Is sex just a question of experience or technique, or a question of how much in love people are? Everything from *The Kama Sutra* to sex hotlines offers suggestions on how to make sex as enjoyable as possible. There are recommendations you can follow to turn the most beautiful "simple thing" in the world into a competitive sport. Do you have sex less than three times a week? Then work on it! Or: You're over 50? Then anyway sex isn't important anymore. These different opinions are more confusing than useful.

Sex is the result of many factors, at least in our experience. How fulfilling sex is in a relationship depends on how that relationship has developed overall. Other influences include lessons from previous relationships, childhood experiences, what sort of parental role models there were, and much more. So, sex can be a whole ball of wool to untangle if the intimacy between a couple leaves something to be desired.

Sex in itself, as a physical act, is indeed simple. But it is complicated by projections, fears, hurts, and the history of our self-development. We are born with all the potential we need for our lives, including the potential for sexuality. Just look at a baby. You will notice curiosity, liveliness, adventure, and joy with which it wants to discover the world. All those traits are also the basis for fulfilled sexuality that this baby will later enjoy as an adult.

This potential is innate. During our socialization and upbringing, however, some things are enhanced, some are diminished, and some are lost. When two adults meet, they meet with different attitudes toward sexuality that might also have been shaped by experiences in past relationships that they want to repeat or, on the contrary, never want to experience again.

So you see, your needs, fears, and wishes when it comes to intimacy and sex are very individual, and the same is true for your partner. Find the sex life that suits you both, no matter what it is. Don't let friends or the media tell you what "perfect sex" means. Go on a voyage of discovery for yourselves, and let us inspire you to ponder the various issues around sex.

Eroticism and sex

Eroticism and sexuality are often used as synonyms, even though they're not. Eroticism describes the sensual and spiritual affection we feel towards other people. It is the stimulus, the initiation of sex. We feel erotic when we walk holding hands, exchange meaningful glances, speak in a certain timbre. Sometimes a soft touch on the back is enough to initiate attraction or even arousal.

If a couple has no sex, there may be two reasons: a lack of security or a lack of eroticism. Reviving erotic gestures may be an effective way of rejuvenating your sex life.

Who is to blame for the lack of sex?

If you blame your partner because nothing has been happening in bed for a while, you have most likely realized that reproach doesn't enhance your sex life. If you blame yourself, it's no different. Because as soon as only one person takes responsibility, the relationship gets into trouble.

The question that takes you further is: What has been lost in our relationship that we have little or no sex? In that way, you meet on equal footing, and you'll find answers and solutions. The reasons often lie in the past—in childhood experiences, parental role models, in earlier sexual experiences and in previous relationships.

Both of you play a part, and there are many ways to avoid sex: a migraine, stress at work, children in the next room, fatigue. You go to bed much earlier or later than your partner. You absolutely have to finish reading this thriller. Other ways to avoid sex include being pushy, making your partner feel guilty, not responding to his or her sexual preferences, or not being able to stop at just cuddling, etc. It's worthwhile to think about what part one is playing, if sex is not fulfilling.

Irene and Victor, for example, didn't have sex for a long time. Victor was quite stressed by his job and suffered from depression. Only the vigilance of the people around him foiled a suicide attempt. When that crisis was over, he blamed Irene for his suicide attempt, because she had stopped sleeping with him. Fortunately, Irene didn't accept these accusations. Still, she felt stressed and ashamed, because in some way or other the accusation hit the nail on the head. As a result, they became even more distant from each other.

Finally, Victor and Irene came to our couples therapy. In the course of the discussion, Victor realized that both of them had contributed to their lack of sex. Both had bitter experiences in their earlier history, causing both of them to be depressed, and this melancholy made it hard for them to find their sexuality. Ultimately, Victor's suicide attempt was a way out of that condition.

Therapy has helped them put aside the question of guilt. They could then meet on a more mature level, share their sad childhood experiences, find common interests, and grow close to each another again.

Security and passion

Everyone has the ability to experience fulfilling and happy eroticism and sexuality. We all want to try new things and grow in our personality, but that requires security above all. Often, sex isn't working because that's what is missing in the relationship: security. And when one partner has an affair, that's always the case.

Usually, however, it begins much earlier. Insecurity arises where emotional distance builds up. For example, if you are immersed in your job, leaving for the office early in the morning and coming home late at night—this not only creates a lack of time for sex, but above all, it leaves you emotionally out of reach for your partner. It is not uncommon for this to result in a vicious cycle: If your partner finds no more room for passion in the relationship, he might look for a different playing field—and so you throw yourself even more into your work or hobby. Or you start an affair.

Maria and Curt developed the classic woman-man scenario. He threw himself into his job; she directed all of her passion towards the children and the household. Their behavior was amplified by the fact that both of their families of origin were extremely dominating, which made them feel even more overwhelmed. There was no more room for intimacy or eroticism. Instead, they blamed each other. At home, the atmosphere became more and more depressing, Curt lived his passion at his job, Maria hers with the children.

When the corset finally became unbearably tight, they sought help through therapy. "It's like a prison that we know from our families of origin. We don't want to repeat that," was their fervent wish. Slowly they learned to face each other again and appreciate one another as man and woman. They realized that being hard on each other had its origin in their childhoods. "A woman's job is children and household, and everything has to be perfect," was Maria's mother's motto. "You have to bring the money home. When the woman has to go to work, it means that the man is a failure. No fun before the work is done," was the maxim Curt inherited from his parents.

Neither of them observed their parents being physical or intimate. On top of that, Maria's father was sexually abusive when she was ten years old, making suggestive remarks and touching her breasts and bottom. Even though her mother noticed it, she patently ignored it. Maria had no chance to develop a healthy sense of her body.

During therapy, she was finally able to talk about all the things she had suppressed for so many years. Both developed fresh ideas to visualize a new way of life for themselves and the children. They gradually changed their understanding of the role they each needed to play. Maria took on a part-time job she enjoyed, and Curt faced a confrontation with his parents, as they naturally criticized her new work.

If both partners are willing to change something in their every-day life, the atmosphere eases. This easing of tension didn't immediately lead to a great sex life for Curt and Maria, but in time they were able to engage each other physically, sit in front of the fireplace reading, touching one another and leaning their heads against each other. After a few months, they finally had sex again.

That's the domino effect. One small step leads to the next. The willingness to examine an issue more closely leads to awareness, and in turn, provides security.

Sex and power struggles

What are relationships without conflicts? A rigid structure with no chance of growth. But sometimes a quarrel can turn into an actual power struggle that eventually leaves its traces even in bed. Here are two possible solutions:

1. A couple gets to the bottom of the conflict together. What's actually behind it? Who feels upset, and why? Most power struggles arise from earlier, unhealed wounds. Whoever manages to find out what's behind the scars and heal them has taken an important step towards solving the actual conflict and reviving their sexuality.

2. Keep the conflict outside. Not all disputes have to do directly with sexuality. Therefore, it's worth the effort to keep it outside the bedroom. That might be difficult,

but in the end quite successful. Physical intimacy releases hormones and messenger substances that facilitate tolerance and commitment--the best conditions for being able to manage conflicts more positively. You don't have to settle the quarrel before having fulfilling sex. The other way around is just as effective.

Joanne and George tried the second option. They had a business together and were in constant conflict about the goals of the company. This led to them no longer having sex. During couples therapy, they realized how great their wish for intimacy was and how they had been punishing each other when they abstained from sex because of their quarrels.

They agreed to try it out. They kept the power struggle out of the bedroom and slept together. Interestingly, after several weeks there was also a change in their professional relationship. Joanne and George described each other as calmer, more cooperative, and more development-oriented than before. They found a new corporate philosophy and common goals. So, they ended up having more fun not only during sex, but also in their work.

Of course, this path doesn't always succeed. If earlier wounds, a profound lack of appreciation or something of that sort gets in the way of sex, you can't just leave it outside and have sex. That brings us to the next point.

Significant wounds and abuse
A lack of sex drive is sometimes associated with sexual assault encountered by one or both partners early in life. Not only rape is considered sexual assault. It might mean lewd looks, ambigu-

ous comments, being touched in intimate places, or even just the touch of a hand combined with a lascivious smile. Sexual assault and rape are the peak of physical and psychological violations. The effects of such severe transgressions are sometimes not recognized until problems arise within a relationship.

It's important not to take the other's dissociative behavior as a rebuke or an affront. Rather, it helps to recognize and respect the other's distress. A person who experiences abuse during childhood not only struggles with insecurity, but also with a great deal of shame. So, they need to feel appreciation, recognition, and the sense that their distress is accepted.

Especially when dealing with traumatic experiences, couples therapy makes sense, as it's challenging to talk about these experiences. A therapist supplies the necessary safe framework for the traumatized person to open up. It takes a lot of courage to trust your partner with previous abuse and assaults.

That is why the partner's reaction is of the utmost importance. If such an issue can be brought up within the relationship, it means that the relationship is sustained by a sense of security. Be grateful that your partner is aware of those early experiences and can talk about them with you, because only through awareness can healing begin. Statements like this would be counterproductive: "Oh, come on, that happened in your childhood! I'm completely different, so let's sleep together." That would only lead to further pain rather than helping to heal.

Rose and Herbert came to therapy because they had difficulty with their sex life. After a few sessions, Rose said how difficult it was for her to open up to Herbert, and meant it literally. "I can't spread my legs and let you enter. My entire body feels stiff as a board." At the same time, she truly loved him and didn't want to put the brakes on his desire. "That's why I keep sleeping with you."

It was incredibly frustrating for Herbert. He wanted nothing more than for his wife to be happy and satisfied. When Rose told him about her difficulties, he cried, because he could feel how uncomfortable and painful it must be for her. In the ensuing conversation between them, Rose remembered a situation with her uncle, who occasionally took care of her and her siblings. When Rose was twelve, he watched her taking a shower, claiming she needed help. He tried several times to convince her that he had to wash her vagina with soap because it would only be clean if he stuck the soap into it. Rose was able to defend herself against having the soap put inside her, even though she wanted to believe this grown man. She was stiff with shame and anxiety, and those feelings never left her body.

During further therapy sessions, both worked at resolving the trauma of this long-ago experience. In addition, Rose showed him the physical contact that triggered her trauma, so that Herbert could be mindful of this in his actions. Rose's confidence increased. After a few weeks, they were able to have sex and to experience an orgasm together.

Now, years later, they have told us that their sex life and intimacy are exceptional. Only on very rare occasions do old memories surface for Rose. Once, Herbert was confused when Rose once asked him to grab her tightly and to be really wild. It unsettled him, but she pointed out that she could differentiate between being at the mercy of someone as a child, and the great sense of security she now felt. With this certainty, she could imagine experiencing just about anything with him.

As you can see, within a relationship, it's possible to heal deep wounds and abuse with a certain amount of time and patience. In the end, sex may be much better than the couple ever dared to imagine. Ultimately, Rose, too, wanted her Herbert to "take her with frenzied emotion." The old traumas were healed, giving way to an intimate, deep passion.

Feedback within physicality

A good relationship, intimacy, and sexuality strongly depend on how you perceive each other, and how willing you are to give and take feedback. For example, if it's difficult for a woman to be sexually attracted to her partner because he's unkempt and reeks of sweat, it would be wrong for her not to mention it out of consideration. She'd only negate her needs and feelings. Of course, she shouldn't say such things crudely. That type of feedback might lead to shame and possible withdrawal.

Feedback is important, and of course, positive feedback is also needed—showing appreciation for what you especially love. Everyone is happy if the new perfume or the sexy t-shirt gets noticed. Just remember the 5:1 rule from Chapter 10. And wishes are also appropriate: "When we go out on dates, I wish you'd get all dressed up for me." Or. "Before we have sex, it's important to me that you've taken a shower within the past twelve hours."

The planned date vs. spontaneous sex

A planned rendezvous for sex can often work wonders, even if many consider it unromantic. It can be especially important to find time for each other when the calendar is full of work and family appointments. Because in everyday life, there usually is time for everything: the job, children, and parents—only eroticism falls by the wayside.

Just knowing you have a date with your husband or wife can be erotic. It awakens anticipation and excitement, and enhances desire and joy. Such dates should be taken seriously and adhered to.

From around the age of forty, the decision-making behavior around sexuality changes. At a younger age, we first experience sexual arousal and then decide to have sex. At around forty, this behavior is usually reversed: We first decide to have sex, and then feel lust and excitement. So, if you are over forty, don't wait until you are sexually aroused, or sex will never happen. Plan it, and then arousal will follow.

Bedroom Sanctuary

Are there any neglected objects or unused pieces of furniture in your bedroom, or other dust traps such as old dried flowers? Then it's no wonder that your sex life leaves something to be desired. Worst of all are photos of laughing children or an entire gallery of ancestors watching you having sex.

Your favorite spot for intimate moments should be lovingly arranged. You will see how a tantalizing photo of your last vacation, dim lights, soft cushions, cozy blankets, and a comfortable temperature can promote the desire for sex. Because who can think about intimacy with scratchy sheets and goose bumps?

Your body

Many want their partner to be sexually open, but have little connection with their own body. It might be because you're unable to touch, feel, look at, or hear yourself. It helps to talk about it, for example, telling your partner how you feel in your skin. Or you invite him to join you on a journey of discovery. If it's difficult for a woman to accept herself as a woman with her breasts, it may be helpful if she stands in front of a mirror with her partner, while he looks into her eyes and says, "Just look at that beautiful woman in the mirror."

How often do you have sex?
We asked an almost 80-year old couple that question. "All too seldom," was the reply. "Only three to four times a week." In contrast, a 40-year-old couple was quite happy with their sex life. How often did they have sex? "Well, about once a month," they guessed.

As you can see, it's not helpful to orient yourself on other couples, or to what the media wants us to believe, or even to a prior relationship. What's more important is gauging and recognizing your desires. This makes it possible to develop something mutual that pleases both partners.

The courage to try something new
Some would like to try something new to bring more variety and fun into their sex life. Or they want to try something new because sex is a problem and they hope to get things moving again. In any case, it takes courage.

The motto is: Don't wait for the other to take the first step, but start with yourself and try to overcome your ambivalence. An example: Connie had already born five children. Sometimes she didn't feel "filled up" when she had sex with her husband, Martin. She was afraid she was "too wide." When she finally mustered the courage to tell Martin about it, both felt quite embarrassed. She felt physically inadequate, and he thought that he was unable to provide her with enough "manhood." Then

Martin had the idea to buy a vibrator. Initially, Connie was embarrassed, but Martin went ahead and bought it, and their sex life took a turn for the better. The vibrator became a "tool" for more physical contact and fulfilled sex.

Sometimes it's hard getting up the courage. Try being open for once: "Listen, I have a hard time telling you this, but it's very important." A bashful smile or a glance can make both of you grin. Feigned courage creates distance, but honest embarrassment can be pretty charming!

Fantasy

Fantasies concerning intimacy and sexuality have an important place in a partnership. Therefore, it's crucial to share these fantasies.

Marion and Erwin, for example, only had sex in the bedroom because of their children. "I'd love to have sex with you on the tram," Marion said, and then broke out laughing because she was shocked at herself. Of course, she'd never really want to do such a thing. But that remark broke the ice. Together they came up with an idea—after so many years—to try it instead in the living room. They asked Grandma to take the kids overnight so they could have the house to themselves.

The first evening they went to the movies. After that, they were so tired that they went to sleep immediately. They asked themselves if the whole thing was ridiculous. So much ado about nothing and more nothing! Still, they repeated the procedure, and by the third try, it worked. After a nice evening at the theater, they had a glass of wine in the living room. One loving gesture led to another, the sparks flew, and they ended up having an erotic night with no wishes left unfulfilled. Marion's fantasy was the driving force from which something entirely different had developed.

What It Was Really About

Sabine and Roland's quarrel on the first evening of their skiing vacation is probably one of the most common couple's issues: One wants sex, the other thinks up reasons to avoid it. A classic power struggle.

Sabine's primary issue was the feeling of having no self-defined space in life. You might remember the story in Chapter 2 concerning the tragic death of Sabine's sister. Sabine's birth was the compensation; she filled a void. It was her duty to make her mother happy instead of just being herself and seen as an individual personality.

"If Roland buys a stereo system without asking me, he pushes exactly the button that makes me feel like there is no space for me. At the same time, I knew it was a good buy. That's probably why I couldn't find the words to express my frustration." The frustration found another channel: The prospect of so much closeness through sex brought the desire for individual space to the foreground.

"Of course, you're not aware of these thoughts. It's more like a reflex. I'm glad that through the years I've learned to express my hurt feelings as quickly as possible. As a respectable turtle, it used to take me months before I was able to talk about something. I'm sure that hindered a lot of beautiful moments in our sex life. Today I'm able to talk about things that bother me within minutes, allowing me to get it over and done with quickly."

Roland learned at an early age to save desires for later. Vacations, or even breakfast with the family—meaning physical closeness—were the reward for hard work. "I learned to suppress my desires. First work, then play. When we finally were able to go on holiday after many months of work, all my neediness emerged. That, of course, put pressure on Sabine and activated her standard behavior pattern. And then I was all the more disappointed."

With the help of therapy, Roland learned not to defer his desires, but to articulate them as soon as they arise. Better communication with Sabine gave rise to a direct and honest connection that gave them both a sense of security. "We have developed a mutual sexuality that we never even dared dream about in the past."

What You Can Do

Individual exercises

- Look for a place where you can relax. Close your eyes and try to figure out how your body feels. How do you experience yourself as a sexual being? Where do you find yourself particularly attractive, and which parts of your body are you dissatisfied with?

Decide on something that increases your body esteem: participate in sports; dress differently; visit a dentist; consult a girlfriend; buy a new dress or underwear.

- Try to remember events in your past that may have hurt your sense of intimacy and sexuality that might have laid the groundwork for your present-day difficulty with living your sexuality. Make a note of the messages your parents conveyed about sexuality. Examples: "Sex is something beautiful." "The only reason for sex is to have children."

🌱 See if you can sense which pictures and feelings emerge when you imagine your parents being intimate and having sex. What was it like when you were a child? What did your mother teach you, what did your father convey? Often, parents don't talk about their own sexuality; their children sense it between the lines, in the atmosphere. Examples: "My mother always said my father only wants one thing, but he doesn't love me." What have you taken from that as a woman? Maybe, "I have to be more reserved with my husband."

Another example: Did you hear from your father that his wife, in this case your mother, "used to be funny, but now she's just uninteresting"? Maybe you gathered from this that women today are rather boring? Think about the ways that your parents' relationship has shaped the structure of your relationship, especially around the topic of intimacy and sexuality.

🌱 What about your partner really bothers you sometimes, but you have never shared it with him or her? Make a list of what's important to you. You might want to let him know that it matters if he takes regular showers; tell her that you like it when she buys new underwear; and so on.

Exercises for Two

🌱 Arrange a date night together. Perhaps there will be a rule like, "Every Friday night belongs to us." If not, suggest this to your partner, and talk about whether such an evening can be arranged.

🌱 Stand in front of a mirror and show your partner the parts you especially love about them. If they react negatively, with aggression or annoyance, then help them out a little by saying, "I love you, and I love these aspects of you especially, because..." Help them to love and appreciate their body.

🌱 Couples with very strong relationships are good at finding a little eroticism in their everyday lives. Give each other daily compliments: "Today, you're looking especially attractive." Or, "The way you're moving around today, I love that so much about you." In any event, these remarks are not meant to encroach on each other, but to increase sexual tension.

🌱 Give each other a mutual massage. If it's too threatening at first—for example, if it's been a long time since you've had sex—begin by massaging with your clothes on. Only later, when you've gotten more comfortable with physical closeness again, try it again naked. While doing this, pay attention to the feedback from your partner. It should be pleasant and relaxing, not a sports massage.

🌱 What do you want to do together to maintain your intimacy and rekindle sexuality? For example, do you want to go together to a reputable erotic shop and get some inspiration from toys? Or would you prefer a special vacation spot where you can relax? Maybe you want to go dancing. Find and exchange ideas that you both like.

🌱 If there is little or no sexuality in your relationship, seek joint conversation, seek dialogue. If possible, start couples therapy. Do you feel secure enough in your relationship to get involved in an experiment? Then agree to lie down together three times for twenty minutes over the next two weeks. Set an alarm and ensure that you can't be disturbed during this time. The first time, lie down on your bed or in some other comfortable place wearing your normal day clothes. The second time, do the same thing, but in your nightclothes, pajamas, or a t-shirt to cover your intimate areas. The third time you will be naked. In these three twenty-minute periods, everything is allowed—laughing crying, being aroused—except sex. That means you touch, cuddle, but you don't grab your wife's breast or your husband's bottom. There are no sexual acts.

🌱 Find all your courage together and tell each other your fantasies about mutual intimacy and sexuality. That doesn't mean the other one has to act on it. Often something new develops out of this that has nothing to do with the original fantasy. So, it is definitely worth it to talk about fantasies even if you're convinced your partner will not like them. Also differentiate between fantasies you really want to try and fantasies that are out of the question for you to implement.

🌱 Examine the nature of the space where your intimate and sexual life unfolds. Is your bedroom a hodgepodge of discarded items? Is it really a nice place, or is it cold and untidy? Design this space together: maybe new satin duvet covers, a small hi-fi system for suitable background music, or a different lamp that provides subdued lighting. Maybe you'll decide to redecorate your bedroom from scratch because it's old.

12. Farewell Instead of Breaking Off

A basis for a new beginning and self-development

Roland and Sabine are on a ski vacation when, after breakfast, while packing their things for the day, Roland declares:
"I don't know how to tell you this, but I've decided to leave you."
Sabine freezes. She's speechless. Stunned, she looks at Roland.
"I can't explain it. All I can say is: I need my freedom and feel you are holding me back. I want you to know that I'm leaving you today."
"Uh, today?" Sabine stammers.
"Yes, today. Once I know I want to leave you, why wait until tomorrow?"
"But only two weeks ago we talked about how nice it is together…"
"That was fourteen days ago…"
Sabine is shocked and doesn't know what to do or how to respond. In her helplessness, she goes along with Roland to meet their friends. On the bus, Roland talks with the others as if nothing had happened. Sabine is still dumbstruck, aimlessly staring out the window, as she watches the landscape passing by. Even on the slopes, she doesn't say anything, while Roland acts like he is having fun. Later, on the ski lift:
"I just don't get it, Roland. What happened? Can you explain it to me?"
"What's there to explain? I want to separate!"

"Yes, but...."

"A separation is a separation. And you don't have to cry. We had a good time, and now I need my freedom."

A Proper Farewell Provides a Basis for Something New

If humans could handle farewells better, we would have a lot more positive energy for shaping our future. We psychotherapists wouldn't have a lot to do if we all were good at separating from the past with respect and dignity.

When we talk about farewells, we don't just mean separation, divorce, or death. Those, of course, are the most tragic with the most severe effects. We are also speaking of a farewell to stressful subjects, from previous hurts that tie up our energy and don't leave space for a positive, constructive future.

For several years now, we have been holding generation workshops, in which a parent participates with a grown child. When asked the question of how the daughters and sons experienced their parents' partnership, more than two-thirds of them answered by pointing out the pressure they felt from their parents' ongoing power struggles, or how they suffered because of undignified separations—undignified because they were characterized by resentment, unfair fights, and mutual attacks.

To separate with dignity and intent gives us the chance to establish a sound basis for a new beginning. People who manage to confront this challenging process are especially successful as individuals and as couples. They become aware of their own actions and learn to take responsibility. And they are rewarded with new, possibly unexpected moments of happiness.

Pain Is a Healing Form of Energy

Bettina and Bertram came to us for couples therapy. Bettina told us that according to doctors, she was terminally ill. They wanted to experience to the fullest the limited time they had left as a couple. They took part in an Imago couples workshop and several of our seminars. When it seemed that Bettina's end was coming, they began—in light of her deteriorating condition—to focus on the approaching death and their farewell. They told us, very touchingly with tears in their eyes, that they were doing a great deal of talking about old times and the beautiful things they had experienced.

In this way, they unconsciously did what is an essential part of farewells: looking back at what was, the good and not so good times, and dreams that, unfortunately, can no longer be realized. Naming it all helps to let it go.

Bettina and Bertram decided to take a last vacation. They traveled to a place where they had had a wonderful time together. They knew that on Monday after the vacation, Bettina had to go into the hospital, and it was pretty much certain that she would never leave the clinic alive. They said goodbye to their life together with dialogues, rituals, and many conversations. Bertram accompanied his wife through her last few weeks and was with her when she died.

Bertram was remarkably composed at Bettina's funeral. He told us it was easier for him to get through the funeral services because he already had experienced a long, intense farewell. Through that long process, which lasted for about a year, the pain at the end wasn't so unbearable and subsided faster.

Nature has provided us with pain as part of a healing process.

Facing that pain frees up enormous potential for energy. When an open wound becomes infected, our body reacts perfectly: It sends energy to the spot which manifests as red, warm, or painful. That energy "repairs" the wound. In this same way, we can heal our emotional wounds: We send our energy wherever something needs to be closed.

The Farewell Dialogue

Whether you're saying goodbye to your partner or to a stressful situation, you are leaving the positive as well as the negative, and the dreams and visions you wanted to achieve. They illuminate your shared history. It's not enough just to keep in mind that the other one was "nice and loving." It's crucial to review exactly what you experienced, in which situations the person was loving, what you felt and saw at such a moment, what was said, what atmosphere you perceived, and so on.

We're taking separate paths

Victoria and Daniel had been entangled in power struggles for months. When Daniel also fell in love with another woman, they decided to separate. They asked us to accompany them through their parting. As in the couples' dialogue, they sat opposite each other and kept eye contact. One person spoke, the other mirrored, and then they switched.

At first, we asked Victoria to think of positive experiences and verbalize them. "I'm saying goodbye to our vacations, like the one in Greece when we spent each evening in our favorite restaurant, ate good fish, and toasted each other with Retsina for good luck. That's over." Of course, such memories give rise to pain and mourning because it's over. But that's the only way to let go. If we hold on to bygones, nothing new can develop.

The next step led Victoria to negative things—not only the negative aspects Daniel had contributed, but Victoria's as well. "I'm saying say goodbye to the time I threw a plate against the wall out of rage, when we argued all night after you told me you were having an affair. That won't happen again." Often we only remember the bad things the other one did, but a relationship is always something equivalent. It's healing to realize that you have both contributed to making things difficult.

The third step of the farewell dialog is looking at the future, the goals and visions that you won't achieve as a couple anymore. "I'm saying goodbye to the dream of growing old together, watching our children grow up and have children of their own, and celebrating Christmases with kids and grandkids. That won't happen." Bidding hopes and dreams farewell often carries the greatest power. If we fail to do it, we'll transfer it all to our next relationship, and it won't be able to properly evolve because there'll be another person accompanying us into the future.

Farewell to the living dead

A farewell in a relationship doesn't necessarily have to mean breaking up. When we support a couple in therapy, we often notice that a relationship has a great deal of potential for a happy future, but old habits are blocking it. These have to be abandoned.

Erica and Fritz wanted nothing more than a child. But although everything was fine from a medical point of view, she couldn't get pregnant. They came into our practice and from the first meeting, we suspected something was bothering Erica. She seemed very serious, sad, and withdrawn.

During couples therapy, she later talked about her mother, who never got over the death of her husband. She lived as if he had never died. The urn with his ashes was on her nightstand. "When I lie in bed, I can still feel him here, talking to me," her mother said. She was a highly intelligent woman, full of life, but at home she acted as if Erica's father were still alive. Erica was ten when he died, and she suffered immensely from this loss. But she was even more burdened by the feeling that she had to support her mother in keeping her illusion alive, to prevent her from breaking down completely.

We had Erica conduct a farewell dialogue with her father, with Fritz taking the role of the father. Erica realized that she had always been afraid someone could suddenly disappear like her father once did. Together with Fritz, she worked on her trust that life means her well. Half a year later, Erica was pregnant.

I'm so furious

Ron and Sandra had both been married before. Now their marriage was at a tipping point, and because they didn't want it to end like their previous marriages, they decided on couples therapy. Ron said that Sandra was always disparaging her first husband. After every phone call—Sandra had a child with her first husband and therefore often had contact with her daughter's father—she was upset and furious, and she transferred that anger into her relationship with Ron, where it didn't belong.

It was clear from this story that she hadn't achieved a sense of closure. Sandra hadn't been able to bid her ex-husband farewell in a positive way, and therefore was not able to find inner peace. The farewell dialogue enabled her to rectify the situation.

You should have stayed with the other guy

Christine and Richard had trust issues. Half a year earlier, Christine had a short affair that she told Richard about. She had ended it to stay with Richard, but the story wasn't really resolved. Richard still felt the hurt inside, and whenever they had a conflict, he criticized her and asked her why she didn't stay with the other guy.

By saying that, Richard voiced his insecurity. At the same time, he kept on hurting Christine with that question. After all, she had committed to Richard. They both conducted a farewell dialogue in which Christine was able to say goodbye her ex-lover. Richard stepped into the role of the ex, which wasn't easy for him. It was especially hard for him to mirror the positive things. But it became clear to him why Christine had to enter into that affair. Because he was able to understand her world better, he gained the confidence that she was happy being with him. After all, she had decided to stay with him even though she had had beautiful experiences with the other man as well. With the help of the dialogue, they were able to create a more stable basis for their relationship.

Forgotten, but not healed

Bridget and Gary were just about to split up. In spite of couples therapy, they couldn't find common ground. Suddenly, a topic arose during a coaching session: their daughter Nicole, who had died at birth. The time after that had been very challenging, but somehow it had also brought them closer together. Since there was the suspicion that the doctors were at fault, they filed a malpractice suit into which they were able to project all of their anger and despair. But mourning fell by the wayside.

After that, they never again mentioned children, and now, three years later, it became clear that something was missing. We suggested they go back and make up for the farewell they had missed for their little daughter. The idea terrified them and they refused. They called back three weeks later: They sensed that it was the farewell process they had feared the most, because their grief had blocked their pleasure and their vital energy. At the same time, they knew they had to go through the process together before being able to split up.

In the course of six sessions, they said goodbye in many touching, intimate dialogues with their dead daughter. And today, some years later, they still visit us in our dialogue room—as a couple! This mutual farewell had opened up completely unexpected perspectives about their future. They now have two healthy, happy children.

Letting Go of Each Other

"I already said my goodbyes," is what some people say when they come to us. When we question that, we discover that they had made the decision themselves and presented the partner with it as a given. They thought that was all there was to it.

You can recognize a harmonious farewell if it's done by mutual agreement. That, of course, can't work if someone dies—in all other cases, a good separation is really only possible if you bid farewell to all the positives, negatives, and the lost vision of your future together with appreciation and by allowing yourselves the necessary time. It's not fair to yourself or to the other one to say: "I've decided to stay with this other man, so goodbye!" If you are the person who wants to split up, maybe you feel everything is already clear to you. Still, there's the risk that you'll drag old issues into the new relationship and in turn, fail to find the happiness you're looking for.

We recognize harmonious farewells by the fact that the partners take the time they need to find a good mutual solution. There is, of course, a trap door in this. If you are the person who wants to keep the relationship, you could draw out the mutual solution for a long time to avoid having to say goodbye. But then you've re-entered a power struggle which doesn't get you anywhere.

Building a new, happy future is the goal. That can only work if you decide mutually withoutlazy compromises, and by engaging in a dignified farewell ritual. Then you'll exit the old relationship as a new person with exciting perspectives and new goals.

Hanna and Frederic came to couples therapy. Frederic wanted to split up because he had been having an affair for a year and wanted to stay with the other woman. Hanna wasn't ready to say goodbye. She was in shock and furious. It took a while before she was willing to engage in the separation process. After ten sessions, they thanked us for our work and ended their relationship with a final ritual.

Two years later, by chance, we met Hanna in a bookshop. We chatted for a while; then, she said: "Let me introduce you to my new husband." Around the corner came— Frederic! His affair didn't work out, because the woman had decided to stay in her old relationship. Half a year after their separation, they had met by coincidence and decided to become good friends. That's how they discovered: There's a new person here in front of me! They fell in love once more and became a couple again.

The time factor

For the one who wants to separate, it can't go fast enough. If you don't want to lose your partner, you want to take all the time in the world. After many years of working with couples, we came up with a kind of formula regarding the amount of time is needed for a good and respectful farewell. The amount of time depends on how long your relationship has lasted. Per year you should figure on four to six weeks for the farewell process. Thus, if you've been together ten years and want to separate, count on about a year before you can be on your separate ways positively with new perspectives. Begin counting the moment one has told the other they wish to separate. No matter how long you've had a secret affair, the time only counts from the moment a separation has become a valid option, and you plan to work on a mutual farewell.

This period is full of intense emotions: anger and despair at the beginning, then the challenging phase, often even doubt, until the final farewell, sorrow, and final release. Of course, some couples have gone through all that in longer or shorter periods. But it seems logical that the longer you have been together, the longer it takes.

What It Was Really About

"Looking back and remembering the scene when I told Sabine without thinking that I wanted to split up, I feel somewhat ashamed. That was a typical Hailstorm, always running away! I couldn't really tell her then what was going on inside me.
"From today's perspective, it was probably fear of too much closeness and too much happiness. I wasn't used to someone paying so much attention to me and giving me as much time as Sabine did. I was alone a lot as a child and had to fend for myself. Suddenly, there was a woman who was there for me all the time. That, apparently, was too much for me."
Roland should have invited Sabine to have a conversation: He should have told her that he wants to separate but doesn't actually understand why. That would have irritated Sabine as well, but in that way, both could have found out what it was that made Roland want to flee.
"I was totally in shock when Roland gave me the unmitigated facts. As a typical Turtle, I wasn't able to react in any way. Today, I know that I reinforced Roland's tendencies to flee. I should have told him that he couldn't just end our long relationship. Even though that might have driven him to flee even faster, I could have signaled: 'OK, you can go, but I want to find a mutual farewell over the next few weeks."
Besides that, Sabine felt ashamed. Her mother had told her: "You can't trust men!" She wanted desperately to prove otherwise.
At that time, Sabine and Roland were still quite young and naïve about how to shape a relationship. Fortunately, they had good friends who didn't give advice, but made sure that they stayed in contact. Two months later they met at a party. On the way

home on the tram, they grew closer again. It was back: their spiritual kinship!

By chance, they ended up with their first couples therapist. They analyzed their behavior patterns and resolved to stick with their relationship from then on. A few months later, they decided to get married.

What You Can Do

🌱 To what or whom do you want to bid farewell to make room for something new in your life? It might be a desk that you've wanted to clear out for a while. It could be ancestral portraits in the bedroom you've meant to get rid of or even people you've forgotten or avoided saying goodbye to.

Ask your partner to help you with this. And offer your help as well. You might want to walk through your home together and think about which things you want to get rid of.

🌱 For the next one or two weeks, convey your appreciation to your loved one before you turn the light off and go to sleep. Let him or her know what it is that you treasure and specifically like about them. Name five things you especially appreciated during the day. Use the present tense: "Today, I appreciate your …" Make sure the last word is positive and loving, so that you can fall asleep with that feeling.

🌱 If you have lost a child with your partner or in a previous relationship, either through miscarriage, abortion, or death, try to feel inside of you if you've really said goodbye. If not, think of a mutual ritual to bid that child farewell with love and appreciation. Then you can have a farewell dialogue (see above), or use the following rituals, for example:

1. Balloon: Fill a balloon with helium and write good wishes on it for your child, and all the dreams, hopes, and visions connected to that child. Go to an elevated place like a small hill and let the balloon fly away, with the idea of freeing that soul.
2. Box: Find symbols and objects that connect you to your lost child. That might be an ultrasound image during pregnancy, clothes you bought for the child, a stone dedicated to that child, a letter, etc. Put those things in a box, close it, and look for a good place to bury it. The idea is to bring closure and lovingly say goodbye to the child, so that your grief transforms into positive energy.

13. Had Children, Built a House, Planted a Tree—What Next?

A relationship needs a medium—and a long-term vision

"You know," Roland said, "I have no idea what our next goal could be. There's that saying: 'A man should build a house, father a son, and plant a tree. We've done all that!"

"You're right. We've renovated this house and have three great kids. We even planted a tree. Well, haven't you always wanted to write a book?"

"That's true, Sabine. When we gave up the family business, I wanted to write a book about it. But the topic doesn't apply anymore."

"So, you have a lot more to say now!"

"Well, if I wanted to write a book, then it'd be with you. And, of course, it should be about relationships."

"Do you think we could really do that?"

"It's not totally crazy! But it's much too much work to look for a publisher. And, who knows if anyone is even interested in that topic."

"Come on! What do you always say? What's your biggest dream?"

"Yes, you're right. Writing a book is really a big dream. But all that effort!"

"Roland, if you really wish for it a hundred percent, then your wish will come true."

"That works for your wishes. Not for mine."

"I bet it'll work for you, too. You'll see."

"OK." Roland closes his eyes and imagines a publisher coming to him and being interested in a relationship book. "I don't think that anyone will really come."

"It won't work like that, Roland. You have to wish for it, and stop the negative thoughts. What do you think? Will a man come, or a woman?"

"Well, I see it very clearly now…I think it's a man, but a woman is there as well."

Some months later, in May, Roland said: "You see, Sabine, my wishing really doesn't work. No publisher has come along!"

"Oh, you'll see…"

One morning in October, Roland arrives at the therapy center, and a man is there waiting for him. "Good morning, Mr. Bösel," he says. "May I introduce myself? My name is Scheriau, and I manage the ORAC publishing house. I heard a lecture you and your wife gave one evening, and I was really impressed. Would you be interested in writing a book?"

Man Strives as Long as He Lives

We hope that Goethe will forgive us for adapting one of his quotations, "Man errs as long as he strives," for our own purposes. It reflects what we have learned in over twenty years of working with couples. As long as we have a vision about our future, our life has a foundation. It's in our nature to have a goal. Only when we know where we want to go do we have an engine that drives us.

Couples who have no vision of their future are in danger. They live alongside each other and dry out, so to speak, or look outwards and search for a shared future with another partner.

We also need a vision for our own lives, independent of the relationship—but if there is no vision for a shared future, an essential pillar is missing.

A mutual vision is more than just the glue keeping you together. We've observed that couples with a clear view of their future have an especially deep bond and commitment to each other. So, we hope you take it to heart and that you and your partner develop a shared vision. Even two completely contrary images can and should, in the end, lead to a common goal.

Growing and learning are the foundations of life

Daily, hourly, even every minute and second we feel the impulse to grow. We are constantly stimulated to learn and try something new, to strive for the next small or large goal. Accomplishing something makes us happy. Just think of how pleased a baby is the first time he stands on his own two legs: He looks proud, content, and joyous. At that moment, many physiological reactions and hormones are emitted in his small body. It's why life is so worth living.

If we don't receive any new growth stimuli or we refuse to acknowledge them, we lose our vitality and our zest for life. A relationship is nourished by growth stimuli from both partners—because what good does it do if only one evolves and the other withdraws? Without that drive, we look for substitute gratifications. Drugs, excessive work, TV addiction, excessive eating, money, and status symbols—all of that consoles us and becomes much too important. It is obvious that all those choices make us sick in the long run. Too much TV or overeating is just a replacement for what we naturally desire: to grow and learn into old age.

In our Imago workshops, we can clearly observe this "wanting to learn." Couples arrive insecure, depressed, afraid, or excited, and say: "I've never been to such a seminar. I don't know anything about psychology, but I want to give us a chance." That's what it's all about—giving the growth impulse a chance. It's our job to create the necessary security in our workshops so that couples can face up to things, try out something new, and dare to say things they never dared saying before. By the next day, their bright faces show that something is already developing. The great about it is that it's not us or the workshop leaders, but the people themselves working toward their happiness.

How Do I Find My Couples Vision?

Basically, it's very simple: two chairs, two people connected by a mutual history, undivided attention, and talking about the biggest dream you'd like to share with your partner. Sketch the vision of your collective future as clearly as possible. Where will you be; what does it look like; who's there; what do you hear; what is your partner doing; what are you doing? It's important to set aside negative ideas about why something can't work out; and don't worry if the two of you have different visions.

With our help, Cathy and Peter found their vision, even though in the beginning, it didn't look like there was any common ground. Cathy's vision was to go abroad for vocational training. Peter wanted to start a family; have children. Two visions which didn't fit together. Together they looked at their backgrounds: Peter's childhood home was shaped by a very strong family life, but vocational training didn't have top priority. It was essential to learn a trade, get a secure job, but a further education wasn't necessary. In Cathy's family, the opposite was true: Her mother had wanted to become an actress, but then Cathy was born and her mother gave up her dream. Cathy wanted to do better. She wanted to achieve her dream job—but she also wanted children.

The following sessions revolved entirely around the family histories of the couple rather than their vision itself. Cathy learned to liberate herself from her mother as a role model and to find her own concept of life. Peter recognized hidden hurdles that stood in the way of his professional development. One day, Cathy finally said: "Why do I have to choose between a job and a child? Please, Peter, help me. I want to do both!" Peter was happy, because he, too, had come to believe that it didn't have to be just the one or the other, but both were possible. Now they were able to work on their shared vision.

Apparent opposites may fit into a shared vision if you take a closer look at your backgrounds and learn from them. Cathy and Peter undoubtedly profited from their wish to develop a shared vision: They solved old patterns and beliefs, freeing themselves for a new way of shaping their lives.

Energy follows attention

Energy develops where we focus our attention. Once we had Rita and Charles in our practice, and Rita always talked about how Charles would probably leave her soon and cheat on her. Charles couldn't assure her often enough that it wasn't so. It didn't help. His wife's distrust upset him and he felt more and more cornered by her accusations, until one day he actually started an affair. "Just to satisfy you. Now I have another woman who loves me and trusts me and doesn't constantly torment me with recriminations," he said during an argument.

That's a typical example of a couple that doesn't have a positive goal for a partnership but a negative one. Rita formulated it as follows: You'll surely leave me. Nevertheless, Charles also contributed to their misfortune. He remained defensive instead of formulating a positive vision, developing it with Rita, and making it a reality.

So please, direct your energy and attention to what you want, not to what you don't want. Various studies show that when we use the word "not" or "none," we confuse our brains. For example, if you say, "I do not want to argue in the future," there's the risk that what the brain receives is the word "argue." Our energy and attention then focus on that word. It would be better to paraphrase the wish not to argue in positive terms. "In the future, I want to talk lovingly and appreciatively with you and discuss our topics constructively."

It's important to be one hundred percent sure of what you truly want, even if in the beginning the vision is still unclear and apparent inconsistencies arise during the exchange. It's worth it to stick to the dialogue until you have described your shared vision clearly and precisely, and you are both absolutely convinced. The more convinced you both are, the more likely it is that your vision will become a reality.

Give your brain and your sensory organs the chance to experience not only your vision with all its nuances, but also everything that can help you along the way. Here is a wise Hasidic saying: "The world is full of miracles, but humans cover them up with their little hands." That's what happens quite often; we miss possibilities and opportunities along the way because we don't look closely enough.

Anna told us that a few years ago she wished she could finally find the right man for her. She had an exact vision of how he should look, what preferences he had—but he didn't appear. One day, she sat next to a longtime co-worker at lunch, and they had a really nice conversation. They even flirted with each other and, on that same day, agreed to go on a date. Today, Anna is still with her Julian, and it makes them smile when they remember that they worked in the same room for three years without noticing one another, even though they were both looking for a partner.

Obstacles

Rose had a clear vision of how her future husband should look: Blond, long hair, slender, tall. But he just didn't wouldn't come. That was at a time when Rose was quite busy with her job. She managed the family business with her brother. Neither was happy in this job, but they felt they had to continue out of loyalty to each other. At some point, her brother finally decided to shut down the company anyway, and when he confronted his sister with that idea, she was much relieved.

On the day the contract to sell the company was signed, Rose went to Switzerland for a wedding. There she met Steve, the brother of the groom, and he was exactly the man she had always dreamed about. Tall, slender, blond—only his hair wasn't long. Still, they became a couple. A few months later, Rose learned that at the time she had visualized her dream man—

about five years earlier—Steve actually had long hair. We leave it up to you to interpret this more closely. We think that back then, Rose wasn't entirely free for that relationship; first, she had to let go of her family responsibilities.

That said, please don't tell your girlfriend all she has to do is to believe strongly enough in her dream, or that she isn't ready if the wish isn't coming true. Something like that is easily said, but doesn't help anyone. On the contrary, it frustrates the person even more.

How Much Luck Do You Deserve?

We humans often limit ourselves—perhaps due to fear of envy or resentment, or because we don't think we have the right to do better than our parents. Nelson Mandela even spoke of this in his inaugural address when he became president of South Africa, that we fear our greatness far more than our inadequacy. But "keeping yourself small doesn't help the world," he continued. Only if we allow ourselves to live our greatness do we allow others do the same.

You might have voices inside you that want to keep you small. Burdensome beliefs are often forced upon us in childhood. "Pride comes before the fall." Perhaps you have dreams and are ashamed because you don't deserve so much luck. "Modesty is a virtue." Just remember what Nelson Mandela said: If you can't accept your greatness and therefore don't fulfill your dreams, you are also holding your partner back from living the greatest possible happiness. Give yourself the chance to break through that inner barrier together.

Trusting instead of tensing up

Christine and Harry had been trying to have a child for a long time, but it wasn't working. They had tried numerous possibilities, even sought the advice of a doctor. They became increasingly tense and gradually lost confidence in their bodies and their relationship. They found they were blaming each other more and more frequently, so they joined our Imago couples workshop. When an attempt at in-vitro fertilization failed, they decided to stop wishing for a child. Accompanied by us, they tearfully bid farewell to their vision of having a future with children. Then they focused on another major project: moving their flower shop to another, better location.

Even though their grief was immense, the sense of closure enabled both of them to relax. Also, something happened in Christine's family to take a great deal of pressure off their shoulders: Christine's sister became pregnant, meaning that the grandchild Christine's parents had long hoped for was on the way. Before that, Christine had felt the entire responsibility for a grandchild, because her siblings either didn't want children or couldn't have any. Now the spell was broken. Two years later we got a call: Christine was six months pregnant and overjoyed.

Of course, you can say that if we are having sex, a baby will be conceived at some point—as long as all biological preconditions are met. But tension is often the greatest obstacle on the way there. We also need confidence and tranquility to make our visions come true.

What It Was Really About

Many years ago, Sabine read the book, *The Cosmic Ordering Service*. At the beginning, she was skeptical, but then she decided to try it out.

"In accordance with the motto, 'if it doesn't help, it won't hurt either,' I tried out small wishes, ordering up a parking space and other little things. It worked! But I was careful, as I didn't want to ruin my good reputation as a serious therapist. So, I didn't tell anyone anything, but was happy when my wishes were fulfilled."

Roland, of course, knew about it, but he was convinced: It works for Sabine, but not for me. "When Sabine reminded me of my wish to write a book, I didn't want to see it as a vision. To be honest, self-constraint lay behind it. How could I write a book when I had such bad grades in German?

"But at some point, I took up Sabine's suggestion and visualized my idea. And, indeed, Mr. Scheriau approached us. We also had conversations with Ms. Pucher, who had assisted us with our writing projects in the past. We knew we were a good team, so we could take Mr. Scheriau up on his offer—and here it is, our book!

"Of course, you could say it would be logical that sooner or later we'd catch a publisher's attention, as we had been in the media quite often over the years. But I'm convinced that ultimately, it was getting rid of my self-restraint and overcoming my fears that people would begrudge us our success. That farewell to fear finally allowed us to tell our personal stories and use them as examples. So, dear readers, we would like to motivate you to stick to it. Find a shared vision and live your couple's dream!"

What You Can Do

For all of the following ideas and questions, it would be good if you first take time for yourself—and wait to exchange your thoughts with your partner later on.

❖ What is your positive vision for your partnership—how do you see your relationship five years from now? Imagine exactly how you and your partner will be living in five years. Where do you live? What do you do? Who is living with you? What kind of job do you have? Do you have children? What will your sex life be like?

❖ What conscious and unconscious dreams have you had in your relationship, and which ones have come true? If visions have already been realized, think about what you did to make that happen. When thinking about your current dreams, keep in mind that some of your visions have already been fulfilled. Use that to support your current visions.

❖ How much luck are you allowed? Try out a mind game: Do you know couples whose happiness you envy? How much of their joy would you allow yourself? The cute kids, yes, but is it just a bit too much that they are successful professionally and able to afford a Porsche? Try to feel where your border lies—that's the barrier you limit yourself with!

❖ Are there people who you think live exactly the way you'd like to live? Take that person, that connoisseur of life, as a role model and consider what you can learn to make your own visions and dreams a reality.

❧ Try new things that seem illogical. For example, instead of following your usual route home from work, take a new route you've never considered before. When brushing your teeth in the morning, try standing on one leg. If you're used to having sex in your bedroom, invite your partner to make love in the living room. As you go down these new avenues, be open to small gifts and surprises. An alternative route to work may take you past a shop where you'll finally find what you've been looking for all along.

Thank You

We thank our parents for their love, their generosity, and everything they've given us for our lives, enabling us to grow and learn and become what we are today: happy and content people. Many thanks to our siblings, who have always supported us.

We especially thank our children Florian, Markus, and Clara, who for many years have given us their trust and love that has endured even in difficult times and taught us a lot.

We thank our dear friends who supported us and were always at our sides, even during the exciting times when we were writing this book.

Of the people accompanying us on our journey, we also want to thank Dr. Zeiler for his love and competence. The same goes for Hedy and Yumi Schleifer, who provided the foundation for our current work as Imago therapists.

Our employees deserve great appreciation for sticking with us and putting up with us, especially Verena Moispointner for her loving and professional support, and Susanne Seper, who acted as office administrator for this book.

A big thank you also goes to Daniela Pucher. This book could only have arisen through capable collaboration in this area of concern. We look forward to working together on future book projects.

We'd like to thank Martin Scheriau and Barbara Köszegi from ORAC-Verlag for suggesting this book and for all the encouragement to keep going.

Last but not least, we thank Maya Kollman, Barbara Bingham, and Kris Krenn for their encouragement and for their help in translating our bestseller into English.

www.kremayr-scheriau.at

ISBN: 978-3-7015-0636-1
Copyright © 2021 by Verlag Kremayr & Scheriau GmbH & Co. KG,
Vienna
All rights reserved.
Dust cover design: Kurt Hamtil
Interior design: Sophie Gudenus
Translation: Kris Krenn, Rachel Miranda Feingold
Copy-editing: Doris Schwarzer
Proofreading: S. R. Ayers
Printed and bound by Florjančič tisk d.o.o., Maribor